Table of Contents

2

Copyright ©
Copyright Protection

Your Free Bonus Gift!

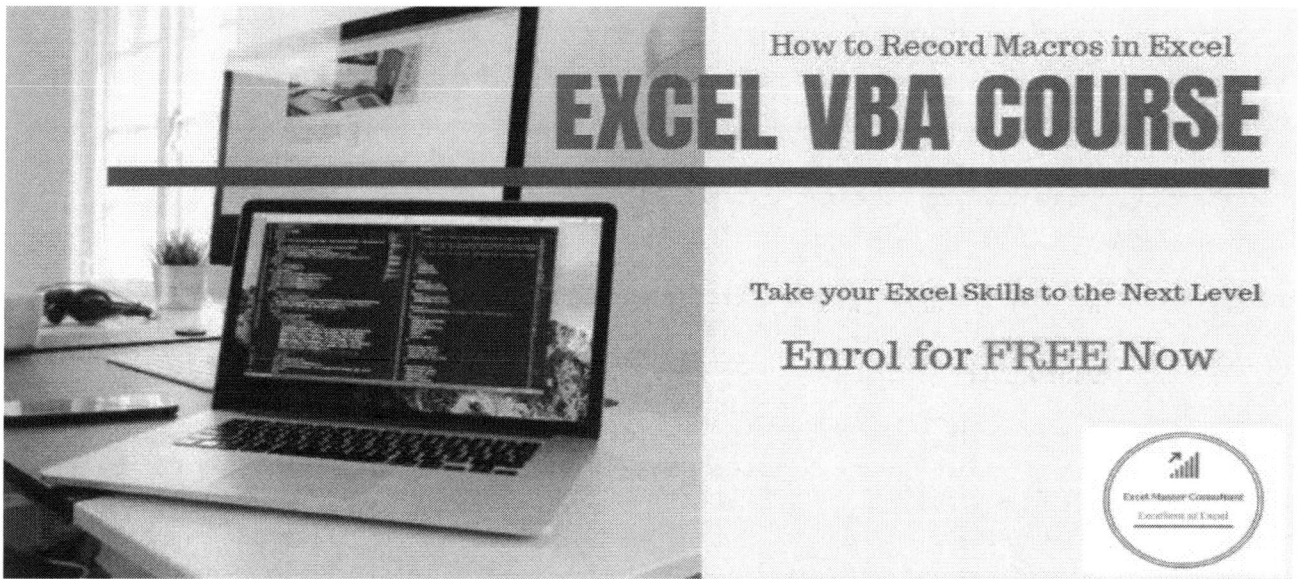

As a small token of thanks for buying this book, I would like to offer a **FREE** bonus gift to all my readers. I am offering a **FREE** online VBA macros course called ***How to Record Macros in Excel***.

In this **FREE** course you will learn:

- How to record a macro to eliminate manual repetitive Excel tasks
- How to execute a macro by:
  - ➢ Using the Macro Dialog Box
  - ➢ Using the Visual Basic Editor
  - ➢ Clicking a button
  - ➢ Clicking a shape

Once you have completed the course you will be able to:

- ➢ Automate Excel tasks easily
- ➢ Save valuable time
- ➢ Advance your Excel skills

You can register for this **FREE** online VBA course by entering the link below to your web browser.

https://bit.ly/2JLFosd

Introduction

Welcome to my Excel Formulas and Functions book!

Microsoft Excel is one of the most widely used software programs in the world, and for good reason. Excel offers a powerful and versatile set of tools for organising and analysing data, creating charts and graphs, and performing complex calculations with ease.

At the heart of Excel's capabilities are its formulas and functions, which allow you to automate calculations, manipulate data, and perform advanced analysis. With the right knowledge of Excel's formulas and functions, you can save time, increase productivity, and make more informed decisions based on the data you collect.

This book is designed to provide a comprehensive guide to Excel's formulas and functions, from basic arithmetic operations to complex statistical analysis. Whether you're a beginner or an advanced user of Excel, this book will help you to enhance your skills and unlock the full potential of this powerful software program.

How will this Book Benefit You?

This Excel Formulas and Functions book is designed to help you develop a deep understanding of Excel's powerful tools for organising and analysing data. By providing a comprehensive guide to Excel's formulas and functions, this book will help you to:

- **Save Time**: By automating complex calculations and data manipulation tasks, you will be able to perform calculations faster and more efficiently, saving time and increasing productivity.

- **Increase Productivity**: By learning how to use Excel's formulas and functions effectively, you will be able to work more efficiently and produce more accurate and reliable results.

- **Analyse Data Effectively**: Excel's formulas and functions can be used to perform complex statistical analysis and data modelling tasks, allowing you to extract valuable insights from your data.

- **Make Informed Decisions**: By using Excel's formulas and functions to perform advanced analysis, you will be able to make more informed decisions based on your data.

- **Enhance Career Prospects**: Proficiency in Excel's formulas and functions is a highly sought-after skill in many industries, and this book will help you to develop the skills and knowledge needed to excel in your career.

Who is this Book Aimed At?

This Excel Formulas and Functions book is aimed at a wide range of readers, from beginners who are just starting to learn Excel to more advanced users who are looking to enhance their skills and knowledge of Excel's formulas and functions.

Specifically, this book is ideal for:

- **Students**: This book is perfect for students who are learning Excel as part of their coursework or who want to develop their Excel skills for future career opportunities.

- **Business Professionals**: Excel is an essential tool for many business professionals, and this book will help readers to master the skills needed to work efficiently and effectively with data.

- **Data Analysts**: Data Analysts use Excel to perform a wide range of tasks, from data cleaning and manipulation to statistical analysis and modelling. This book will provide valuable insights into Excel's formulas and functions that can help Data Analysts to perform their tasks more effectively.

- **Financial Analysts**: Financial Analysts use Excel extensively to analyse financial data, create financial models, and perform financial forecasting. This book will provide valuable insights into Excel's financial formulas and functions that can help Financial Analysts to perform their tasks more effectively.

- **Researchers**: Researchers use Excel to organise and analyse data in many different fields, including science, engineering, and social sciences. This book will provide valuable insights into Excel's formulas and functions that can help researchers to analyse their data more effectively.

Version

This Excel Formulas and Functions book uses the latest version of Excel, ensuring that readers have access to all the latest tools and features that Excel has to offer. The book has been written using Excel 365, which is the most recent version of Excel at the time of writing. This means that readers will be able to follow the examples and tutorials in the book using the most up-to-date version of Excel, ensuring that they can take full advantage of all the latest features and capabilities of the software. Whether readers are new to Excel or experienced users, this book will help them to stay up-to-date with the latest tools and techniques for working with data in Excel.

Two Free Downloadable Excel Workbooks

This book includes two free workbooks; one workbook that includes all the data and the formulas used in the book, and another workbook that contains only the data. This is a great tool for practicing and experimenting with the formulas and functions taught in the book. With this resource, learners can get hands-on experience and build their Excel skills by working through the different exercises and problems included in the book. With these two free workbooks, learners can build their proficiency in Excel and take their skills to the next level. You can download the two Excel workbooks by entering the link below to your browser:

https://bit.ly/3KSPIhP

Contact me on my Website

I have a website dedicated to Excel which is www.excelmasterconsultant.com where readers can find more resources and information to enhance their Excel skills. My website is a valuable resource for anyone looking to improve their Excel skills, from beginners to advanced users. It offers a variety of Excel tutorials, tips, and tricks, as well as online courses to help readers get started with their projects. Additionally, readers can contact me through the website to ask questions or provide feedback on the book or the website. I look forward to hearing from readers and helping them to excel in their use of Excel!

The website again is:

www.excelmasterconsultant.com

Now, if you're ready to take your Excel skills to the next level and become a master of spreadsheet calculations, then let's dive in!

Excel Formulas and Functions Basics

Before we learn about all the different Excel functions that are available and how to create formulas in your worksheets, you first need to understand the basics. In this section, you will learn all the fundamentals of Excel formulas and functions.

What is an Excel Formula?

An Excel formula is a set of instructions that you enter into a cell in an Excel spreadsheet to perform a specific calculation or to manipulate data in a certain way. Excel formulas always start with an equal sign (=) and can be entered directly into a cell or using the formula bar. Excel formulas can include mathematical operators, cell references, functions, and other elements that allow you to perform calculations, manipulate data, or create conditional statements based on specific criteria. Excel provides a wide range of built-in functions that you can use to simplify complex calculations and manipulate data in various ways. Examples of Excel formulas include SUM, AVERAGE, IF, VLOOKUP, COUNTIF, and many more. You will learn about these and more later in this book.

How to Create a Basic Excel Formula

To create a basic Excel formula, follow these steps:

Step 1: Open Microsoft Excel and create a new spreadsheet.

	A	B	C	D
1	10	5		
2				
3				

Step 2: Enter the data you want to use in your formula. For example, let's say you want to add together the values in cells A1 and B1. Enter the values in those cells as shown above.

Step 3: Select the cell where you want to display the result of your formula. For example, if you want to display the result in cell C1, select that cell.

CONCATENATE ▼		✕ ✓ f_x	=		
	A	B	C	D	E	F
1	10	5	=			
2						

Step 4: Begin your formula by typing an equal sign (=) in the selected cell.

CONCATENATE		▾	⋮	✕	✓	f_x	=A1	

◢	A	B	C	D	E	F
1	10	5	=A1			
2						

Step 5: Type or select the cell reference for the first cell you want to add. For example, to add the value in cell A1, type or select cell A1.

CONCATENATE		▾	⋮	✕	✓	f_x	=A1+	

◢	A	B	C	D	E	F
1	10	5	=A1+			
2						

Step 6: Type a plus sign (+) to indicate that you want to add another cell.

CONCATENATE		▾	⋮	✕	✓	f_x	=A1+B1	

◢	A	B	C	D	E	F	G
1	10	5	=A1+B1				
2							

Step 7: Type or select the cell reference for the second cell you want to add. For example, to add the value in cell B1, type or select cell B1.

Step 8: Press **Enter** to complete the formula.

C1		▾	⋮	✕	✓	f_x	=A1+B1	

◢	A	B	C	D	E	F	G
1	10	5	15				
2							

The result of your formula will now be displayed in the selected cell. The formula "**=A1+B1**" will display the result 15 in cell C1.

Congratulations, you've created a basic Excel formula that adds cell references together and displays the result. After you have read this book, you will be able to create more complex formulas using a variety of arithmetic operators and functions to perform calculations on your data.

Using Different Methods to Enter Excel Formulas

There are several ways to enter a formula in Excel, including:

1. Typing the Formula Directly into the Cell

This involves typing the formula directly into the cell preceded by an equals sign (=). For example, to add the numbers in cells A1 and B1, you would type "=A1+B1" into the cell where you want the result to appear.

2. Using the Formula Bar

The formula bar is located at the top of the Excel window and displays the contents of the active cell. To enter a formula using the formula bar, click on the cell where you want the result to appear, type the formula into the formula bar, and press Enter. For example, you could click on cell C1, type "=A1+B1" into the formula bar, and press Enter.

3. Using the Insert Function Dialog Box

This method involves using the Insert Function dialog box to select the function you want to use and then entering the arguments for the function. To use this method, click on the cell where you want the result to appear, let's say cell C1.

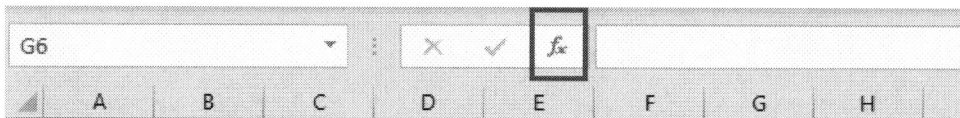

Click on the "Insert Function" button which is to the left of the formula bar as shown above.

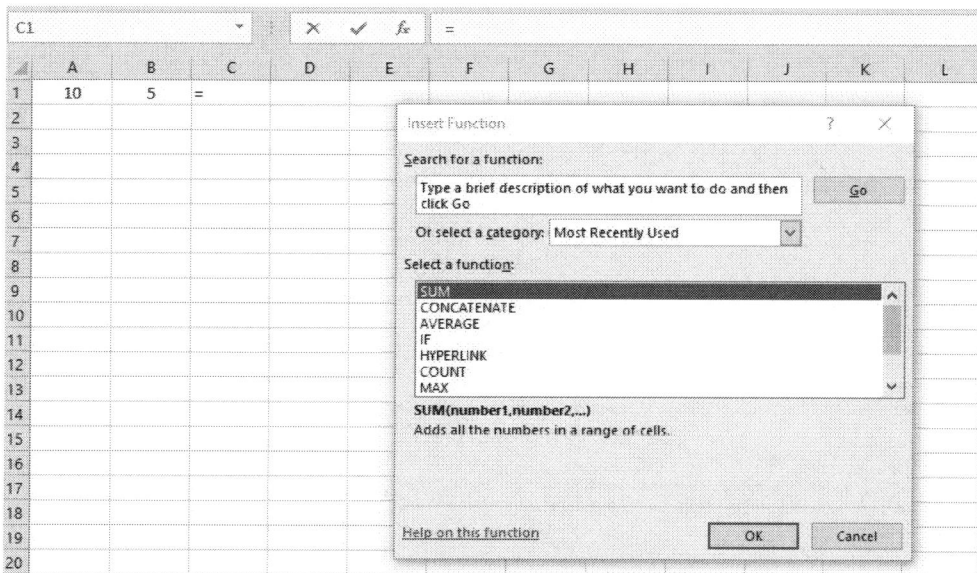

Select the function you want to use. In this example, I want to use the SUM function so I select this and then click on the OK button.

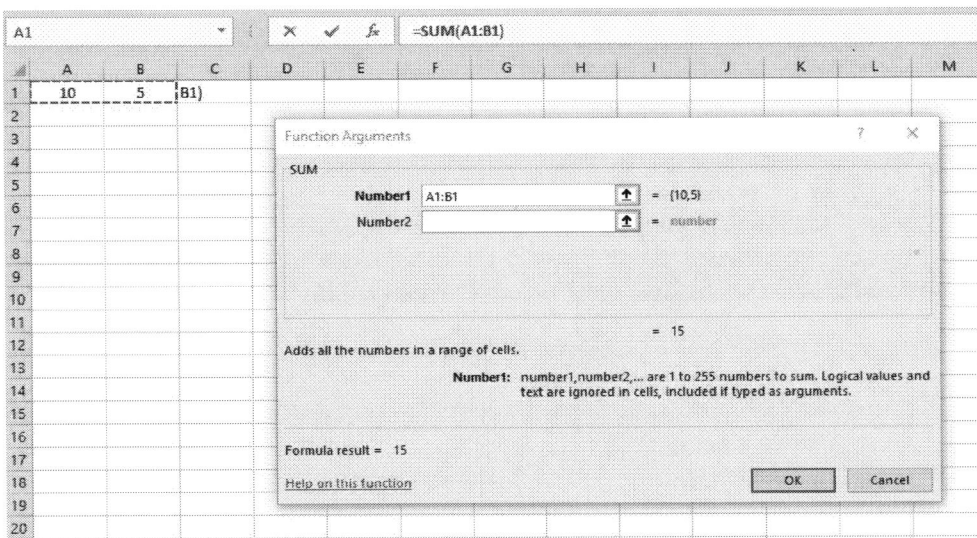

Follow the prompts to enter the arguments. For example, if you want to sum cells A1 and B1, then select this range in the Number1 argument field and then press the OK button. The result will be displayed in the selected cell.

4. Copying and Pasting a Formula

If you have already entered a formula in one cell and want to use it in another cell, you can copy and paste the formula. To do this, select the cell containing the formula and then press Ctrl+C to copy it. Next, select the cell where you want the formula to appear, and then press Ctrl+V to paste it.

What is an Excel Function?

An Excel function is a predefined formula or operation that performs a specific task in Microsoft Excel. It is a built-in feature of Excel that simplifies complex calculations and saves time for users. Excel functions can be used to perform arithmetic operations, manipulate text, extract data, perform statistical analysis, and much more.

Excel functions can be found in the Formula tab under the Function Library group in the Ribbon, and they can also be typed directly into a cell. Some examples of commonly used Excel functions include SUM, AVERAGE, IF, VLOOKUP, and COUNT. Each function has its own syntax and set of arguments, which must be entered correctly for the function to work properly. Later in this book, you will learn about all the best and most commonly used Excel functions and how to apply them to your worksheets.

Excel Operators

In Excel, operators are symbols or characters that are used to perform mathematical, logical or reference operations on values or cell references within a formula. Here are some common examples of operators in Excel and their meanings:

1. Arithmetic Operators:

- Addition (+): adds two or more values.
- Subtraction (-): subtracts one value from another.

12

- Multiplication (*): multiplies two or more values.
- Division (/): divides one value by another.
- Exponentiation (^): raises a value to a power.

2. Comparison Operators:

- Equal to (=): tests if two values are equal.
- Not equal to (<>): tests if two values are not equal.
- Greater than (>): tests if one value is greater than another.
- Less than (<): tests if one value is less than another.
- Greater than or equal to (>=): tests if one value is greater than or equal to another.
- Less than or equal to (<=): tests if one value is less than or equal to another.

3. Logical Operators:

- AND: returns TRUE if all the conditions are TRUE.
- OR: returns TRUE if any of the conditions are TRUE.
- NOT: returns the opposite of a logical value.

4. Reference Operators:

- Range operator (:): creates a range of cells between two cell references.
- Intersection operator (space): returns the intersection of two ranges.

Example:

Suppose you want to test if the value in cell A1 is less than the value in cell B1. To do this, you would use the less than operator "<" in the formula "=A1<B1". The formula will return either TRUE if the value in cell A1 is less than B1 or FALSE if the value in cell A1 is larger than the value in cell B1.

Here is another example. Suppose you want to calculate the average of the values in cells A1 to A5. You can use the AVERAGE function with the range operator as follows: "=AVERAGE(A1:A5)". This formula uses the arithmetic operator (:) to create a range of cells from A1 to A5. The AVERAGE function will then calculate the average of the values in that range.

How to Copy Formulas to Other Cells

There are several ways to copy and paste Excel formulas in a worksheet. Here are some of the most common methods:

1. Using the Ctrl+C and Ctrl+V Keyboard Shortcuts
   1. Select the cell with the formula you want to copy.
   2. Press "Ctrl + C" to copy the formula.
   3. Select the cell(s) where you want to paste the formula.
   4. Press "Ctrl + V" to paste the formula.

2. Using the Fill Handle to Copy a Formula to Adjacent Cells

1. Select the cell with the formula you want to copy.
2. Move the mouse pointer to the bottom-right corner of the selected cell until it turns into a small black cross.
3. Click and drag the fill handle over the cells where you want to copy the formula.

3. Using the Copy and Paste Commands

1. Select the cell with the formula you want to copy.
2. Click the "Copy" button in the "Clipboard" group of the "Home" tab on the ribbon or press "Ctrl + C".
3. Select the cell(s) where you want to paste the formula.
4. Click the "Paste" button in the "Clipboard" group of the "Home" tab on the ribbon or press "Ctrl + V".

4. Using the Paste Special Command to Copy Formulas with Different Formatting or Values

1. Select the cell with the formula you want to copy.
2. Click the "Copy" button in the "Clipboard" group of the "Home" tab on the ribbon or press "Ctrl + C".
3. Select the cell(s) where you want to paste the formula.
4. Click the "Paste Special" button in the "Clipboard" group of the "Home" tab on the ribbon.
5. Choose "Formulas" from the list of options.

5. Using the Ctrl+D and Ctrl+R commands

1. Select the cell containing the formula you want to copy.
2. Select the cells where you want to copy the formula down including the cell that contains the formula.
3. Press Ctrl+D to copy the formula down or Ctrl+R to copy it across.

Relative and Absolute Cell References

In Excel, a cell reference is a specific identifier used to locate and retrieve data from a particular cell or range of cells within a spreadsheet. Cell references are used in formulas and functions to perform calculations, comparisons, and other operations. A cell reference consists of both a column reference and a row reference, which are used to identify the location of a cell in a worksheet.

The column reference in a cell reference is identified by a letter that corresponds to the column heading at the top of the worksheet. Columns in Excel are labelled with letters starting from A and continuing to Z, and then starting again with AA, AB, AC, and so on. Each column in Excel has a unique letter that identifies it. The row reference in a cell reference is identified by a number that corresponds to the row heading on the left side of the worksheet. Rows in Excel are numbered starting from 1 and continuing to 1,048,576. Each row in Excel has a unique number that identifies it.

To create a cell reference in Excel, you need to specify both the column and row references. For example, the cell reference for the cell in column B and row 3 would be B3. Similarly, the cell reference for the cell in column C and row 5 would be C5. You can use cell references in formulas to perform calculations on the data in different cells.

There are three types of cell references in Excel: relative, absolute and mixed.

Relative Cell Reference

Relative cell references are references that change when you copy or move a formula from one cell to another. In other words, when you use a relative cell reference in a formula, it refers to a cell relative to the location of the formula.

| D1 | | | | ▼ | ⋮ | ✕ | ✓ | *fx* | =SUM(A1:C1) |

◢	A	B	C	D	E	F	G	H
1	10	20	30	=SUM(A1:C1)				
2	40	50	60					
3	70	80	90					
4								

Let's say we want to add up the values in the first row in columns A to C. We can use the SUM function in cell D1 with a relative cell reference like this "**=SUM(A1:C1)**".

| D2 | | | | ▼ | ⋮ | ✕ | ✓ | *fx* | =SUM(A2:C2) |

◢	A	B	C	D	E	F	G
1	10	20	30	60			
2	40	50	60	150			
3	70	80	90				
4							

When we copy this formula to the next row, the cell reference adjusts accordingly, so the formula in cell D2 would become "**=SUM(A2:C2)**".

Absolute Cell Reference

Absolute cell references, on the other hand, remain fixed and do not change when you copy or move a formula. When you use an absolute cell reference in a formula, it always refers to the same cell, regardless of the location of the formula. An absolute reference is indicated by placing a dollar sign ($) before the column letter and row number of the cell reference.

◢	A	B	C	D
1	10	20	30	
2	40	50	60	
3	70	80	90	
4	120			
5				

Suppose we have the total of the values in the first column in cell A4 which is 120, and we want to divide each cell value in that column by the total and enter the results in column D.

SUM				▼	⋮	✕	✓	f_x	=A1/$A$4

◢	A	B	C	D	E	F	G
1	10	20	30	=A1/$A$4			
2	40	50	60				
3	70	80	90				
4	120						
5							

We can use an absolute cell reference for the total value like this =$A$4. The formula in cell D1 would be "**=A1/$A$4**".

D2				▼	⋮	✕	✓	f_x	=A2/$A$4

◢	A	B	C	D	E	F	G
1	10	20	30	0.083333			
2	40	50	60	0.333333			
3	70	80	90				
4	120						
5							

When we copy this formula to the next row, the cell reference to the total remains the same, so the formula in cell D2 would be "**=A2/$A$4**". When the cell reference is copied to the third row in cell D3, the formula would be "**=A3/$A$4**".

Mixed Cell Reference

A mixed reference combines both relative and absolute references, and it allows you to create formulas that can be copied to different cells without having to manually adjust the references.

A mixed cell reference can be created by using the dollar sign ($) to fix either the column or row in a reference while allowing the other part to change. For example, if you want to fix the column reference but allow the row reference to change, you would use a mixed reference like this: $A1. This means that the column reference will always refer to column A, but the row reference will change when the formula is copied to other cells.

Similarly, if you want to fix the row reference but allow the column reference to change, you would use a mixed reference like this: A$1. This means that the row reference will always refer to row 1, but the column reference will change when the formula is copied to other cells.

Named Ranges

In Excel, a named range is a defined name given to a specific cell or range of cells. Named ranges are important because they make it easier to refer to a specific cell or range of cells in your formulas.

Instead of referring to cells by their coordinates (e.g., A1:B10), you can give the range a name (e.g., SalesData) and then refer to it in your formulas using the name (e.g., =SUM(SalesData)). This makes your formulas easier to read and understand, especially when working with large and complex spreadsheets.

Named ranges also make it easier to update your formulas if the range of cells changes. For example, if you have a formula that uses the range A1:B10 and you later insert a row at the top of the spreadsheet, you would need to update the formula to use the range A2:B11. However, if you had given the range a name (e.g., SalesData), you would not need to update the formula - Excel would automatically adjust the range to include the new row.

How to Create a Named Range

Here are step-by-step instructions on how to create a named range in Excel:

Step 1: Select the cells you want to name. These cells can be in a single column, row, or multiple columns and rows.

Step 2: Click on the **Formulas** tab on the ribbon at the top of the Excel window.

Step 3: Click on the **Define Name** button in the **Defined Names** group. This will open the **New Name** dialog box.

Step 4: In the **Name** field, type a name for the range. Make sure to use a name that is descriptive and easy to remember.

Step 5: In the **Scope** field, select the option that determines the range's visibility. **Workbook** will make the range visible throughout the entire workbook, while **Sheet** will make it visible only within the current worksheet.

Step 6: In the **Refers to** field, you can either enter the cell or cell range you want to name or use the mouse to select the cells by clicking and dragging over them.

Step 7: Click the **OK** button to create the named range.

The Rules of Creating a Named Range

When creating named ranges in Excel, there are several rules that you need to follow:

- The name must begin with a letter or underscore character. It cannot begin with a number or any special characters.

- The name can contain letters, numbers, and underscore characters only. No other special characters, such as spaces or periods, are allowed.

- The name cannot be the same as a cell reference. For example, you cannot name a range "A1" because it is a cell reference in Excel.

- The name must be unique within the workbook. You cannot have two named ranges with the same name in the same workbook.

- The name cannot be a reserved word in Excel. For example, you cannot name a range "IF" or "SUM" because these are reserved words used by Excel's functions and formulas.

- The name should be descriptive and easy to remember. This will make it easier for you to use the named range in your formulas and functions.

Excel Shortcuts for Named Ranges

In Excel, there are several shortcuts you can use to create and manage named ranges:

- To create a named range quickly, select the cell or range of cells you want to name, and then press **Ctrl + Shift + F3**. This will open the **Create Names from Selection** dialog box, where you can specify the name you want to use for the range.

- To edit an existing named range, press **Ctrl + F3**. This will open the **Name Manager** dialog box, where you can select the named range you want to edit and make changes to its definition.

- To use a named range in a formula or function, type the name of the range directly into the formula or function. Excel will automatically recognise the name and use the range in the calculation.

- To navigate to a named range quickly, press **F5** to open the **Go To** dialog box. Then, select the named range from the **Named Range** dropdown list and click **OK**. Excel will take you directly to the named range.

- To delete a named range, press **Ctrl + F3** to open the **Name Manager** dialog box. Then, select the named range you want to delete and click the **Delete** button.

Now that you know the fundamentals of Excel formulas and functions, let's start to create some formulas of our own using the many functions Excel has available.

Lookup Functions

In Excel, lookup functions are formulas that allow you to search for a specific value in a table or range of cells and return a related value based on the location of that value. There are several lookup functions available in Excel which we will explore in this chapter. Lookup functions are very useful in Excel when you need to quickly find and retrieve data from a large table or dataset. They can also be used to create dynamic formulas that automatically update as the data in your spreadsheet changes.

VLOOKUP Function

What is it?

VLOOKUP is a function in Microsoft Excel that allows you to search for a specific value in a table or range of cells, and return a corresponding value from a different column in that same table. It is one of the most commonly used functions in Excel for data analysis and lookup tasks. The V stands for Vertical.

Syntax

=VLOOKUP(lookup_value, table_array, column_index_num, [range_lookup])

Arguments

- **lookup_value** (required): This is the value that you want to look up in the first column of the table or range of cells.

- **table_array** (required): This is the range of cells that contains the data you want to search. The first column of the range should contain the lookup value, and the data you want to return should be to the right of the lookup column. The table can be a range of cells, a named range, or a table reference.

- **col_index_num** (required): This is the column number (starting from 1) in the table or range of cells that contains the data you want to return.

- **range_lookup** (optional): This argument can be either TRUE or FALSE. If TRUE or omitted, it means the function will search for an approximate match of the lookup value. If FALSE, it means the function will search for an exact match of the lookup value.

Example:

Let's say you have a table of sales data that looks like this:

	A	B	C	D
1				
2		Product	Sales	
3		Apples	$100	
4		Bananas	$75	
5		Oranges	$50	
6		Grapes	$25	
7				

You want to find out how much money was made from selling bananas. You can use VLOOKUP to do this. Below are step-by-step instructions on how to do this:

Step 1: Select a cell where you want to display the result of the VLOOKUP formula. In this example, I select cell F3.

F3				×	✓	f_x	=VLOOKUP(E3,B2:C6,2,FALSE)		

	A	B	C	D	E	F	G	H
1								
2		**Product**	**Sales**					
3		Apples	$100		Bananas	$75		
4		Bananas	$75					
5		Oranges	$50					
6		Grapes	$25					
7								

Step 2: Type the VLOOKUP formula "=**VLOOKUP(E3,B2:C6,2,FALSE)**" in the selected cell.

Here is a breakdown of how the formula works:

- The lookup value is "Bananas" in cell E3. This is the value that we want to find in the first column of the table array.

- The table array is B2:C6, which contains the lookup value in the first column and the sales data in the second column.

- The column index number is 2. This is the column number (starting from 1) in the table array that contains the data we want to return. Since the sales data is in the second column of the table array, we specify 2 for the column index number.

- The range lookup is FALSE. This argument specifies whether we want an exact match or an approximate match. In this case, we want an exact match, so we set the range lookup to FALSE.

- The VLOOKUP formula then searches for "Bananas" in the first column of the table array and returns the corresponding value from the second column.

Step 3: Press **Enter** to execute the formula. The result of this formula would be $75, since "Bananas" is found in the second row of the table array, so the formula returns the value from the second column of that row.

Note: If the lookup value is not found in the leftmost column of the table, VLOOKUP will return an #N/A error.

To Summarise

VLOOKUP is a very useful function in Microsoft Excel that allows you to search for a specific value in a table or range of cells, and return a corresponding value from a different column in that same table. By using the VLOOKUP formula, you can quickly and easily retrieve data from large tables, without having to manually search for the data yourself. The syntax of the VLOOKUP formula consists of four main arguments, including the lookup value, table_array, col_index_num, and range_lookup, which all work together to help you find the data you need. With its powerful capabilities and ease of use, VLOOKUP is a valuable tool for anyone who needs to analyse or work with data in Excel.

HLOOKUP Function

What is it?

HLOOKUP is a function in Microsoft Excel that is used to search for a specific value in the top row of a table, and then return the value from a cell in the same column from a row specified by the user. The H stands for Horizontal.

Syntax

=HLOOKUP(lookup_value, table_array, row_index_num, [range_lookup])

Arguments

- **lookup_value** (required): This is the value that you want to search for in the top row of the table. It can be a value, a reference to a cell, or a text string enclosed in double quotation marks.

- **table_array** (required): This is the range of cells that makes up the table. It must include the top row that contains the lookup value, as well as the row that contains the result that you want to return. The table can be a range of cells, a named range, or a table reference.

- **row_index_num** (required): This is the row number within the table array from which to return a value.

- **range_lookup** (optional): This is an optional argument that specifies whether to perform an approximate match or an exact match. If this argument is omitted or set to TRUE, an approximate match is performed, and the function returns the nearest match to the lookup value that is less than or equal to it. If this argument is set to FALSE, an exact match is performed, and the function returns the value from the exact cell that matches the lookup value.

Example:

Below we have a table of grades for three students.

	A	B	C	D	E	F	G
1							
2			Math	Science	English	History	
3		Student A	75%	80%	85%	90%	
4		Student B	85%	90%	95%	85%	
5		Student C	90%	75%	80%	95%	
6							

We want to return the grade for student A for Math. Below are step-by-step instructions on how to do this using the HLOOKUP function:

Step 1: Select a cell where you want to display the result of the HLOOKUP formula. In this example, I select cell I2.

	A	B	C	D	E	F	G	H	I
1									
2			Math	Science	English	History		Math	75%
3		Student A	75%	80%	85%	90%			
4		Student B	85%	90%	95%	85%			
5		Student C	90%	75%	80%	95%			
6									

Formula bar: I2 — fx — =HLOOKUP(H2,C2:F5,2,FALSE)

Step 2: Type the HLOOKUP formula "**=HLOOKUP(H2,C2:F5,2,FALSE)**" in the selected cell. This formula searches for the value "Math" in row 1 of the table C2:F5 and returns the value from the second row (which is the grade for Math for student A in this case).

Let's break down this formula:

- The first argument, "Math" in cell H2, is the value that we are searching for in the first row of the range C2:F5.

- The second argument, C2:F5, is the range of cells that we want to search in.

- The third argument, 2, specifies that we want to return the value from the second row of the range. This means that when "Math" is found in the first row, the function will return the corresponding value from row 2.

- The fourth argument, FALSE, tells the function to only return an exact match for the search value. This means that if "Math" is not found in the first row of the range, the function will return an #N/A error value.

Step 3: Press **Enter** to execute the formula. The result should be the value 75%, which is the grade for Math in row 2 of the table.

You can now use this same formula with different search values to retrieve grades for other subjects from the same table.

To Summarise

The HLOOKUP function in Excel is a powerful tool that allows you to search for a value in the top row of a table or range, and then return a corresponding value from a specified row within that range. By following the steps outlined above, you can easily use the HLOOKUP function in your own Excel spreadsheets to retrieve specific data based on search criteria. Whether you're working with grades, sales data, or any other type of data that is organised in rows and columns, the HLOOKUP function can help you quickly and efficiently find the information you need.

XLOOKUP Function

What is it?

XLOOKUP is a powerful function in Microsoft Excel that allows you to search for a value in a table or array and return a corresponding value in the same row, column or intersecting cell. It is a new and improved version of the VLOOKUP and HLOOKUP functions, which can be used in more flexible ways and has several additional features.

Syntax

=XLOOKUP(lookup_value, lookup_array, return_array, [if_not_found], [match_mode], [search_mode])

Arguments

- **lookup_value** (required): The value or cell reference you want to search for in the lookup_array. This argument can be a value, a cell reference, or a formula that returns a value or reference.

- **lookup_array** (required): The array or range of cells where you want to search for the lookup_value. This argument can be a range of cells or an array constant, which is a set of values enclosed in curly braces.

- **return_array** (required): The array or range of cells containing the values you want to return. This argument can be a range of cells or an array constant.

- **if_not_found** (optional): The value or action to take if the lookup_value is not found in the lookup_array. This argument can be a value, a cell reference, or a formula that returns a value or reference. By default, if_not_found is set to #N/A, which returns the #N/A error message if the lookup_value is not found.

- **match_mode** (optional): A number that specifies the type of match to be performed. This argument can be set to 0, 1, or -1. If match_mode is omitted, XLOOKUP will assume an exact match (0). Here are what the numbers mean:

    - 0 (default): Exact match.

    - 1: Exact match or next smaller item (when lookup_value is larger than any value in the lookup_array).

    - -1: Exact match or next larger item (when lookup_value is smaller than any value in the lookup_array).

- **search_mode** (optional): A number that specifies the type of search to be performed. This argument can be set to 1 or 2. If search_mode is omitted, XLOOKUP will assume a search from top to bottom, then left to right (1). Here are what the numbers mean:

    - 1 (default): Search from top to bottom, then left to right.

    - 2: Search from bottom to top, then right to left.

Example:

Let's say you have a table with employee information, and you want to find an employee's salary based on their ID number. Here's what the data might look like:

▲	A	B	C	D	E	F
1						
2		ID	Name	Department	Salary	
3		101	John Smith	Marketing	$60,000	
4		102	Jane Doe	Sales	$75,000	
5		103	Bob Johnson	IT	$80,000	
6		104	Sarah Lee	Finance	$70,000	
7						

Suppose you want to look up the salary for ID 101. Below are the steps to achieve this using the XLOOKUP function:

Step 1: Select a cell where you want to display the result of the XLOOKUP formula. In this example, I select cell H3.

H3		× ✓ f_x	=XLOOKUP(G3,B2:B6, E2:E6)				

▲	A	B	C	D	E	F	G	H
1								
2		ID	Name	Department	Salary			
3		101	John Smith	Marketing	$60,000		101	$60,000
4		102	Jane Doe	Sales	$75,000			
5		103	Bob Johnson	IT	$80,000			
6		104	Sarah Lee	Finance	$70,000			
7								

Step 2: Type the XLOOKUP formula "**=XLOOKUP(G3,B2:B6, E2:E6)**" in the selected cell.

Here's how the XLOOKUP formula works:

- The first argument cell G3 is the lookup value "101", which is the value we want to find in the lookup array.

- The second argument B2:B6 is the lookup array, which is the range of cells that contains the lookup value. In this case, it's the ID column of the employee table.

- The third argument E2:E6 is the return array, which is the range of cells containing the values we want to return. In this case, it's the Salary column of the employee table.

- When Excel executes the formula, it searches for the lookup value "101" in the lookup array B2:B6.

- If it finds an exact match, it returns the corresponding value from the return array E2:E6. In this case, it finds an exact match for "101" in cell B3, and returns the corresponding salary value $60,000 from cell E3.

- If it doesn't find an exact match, it returns an error. However, you can use the optional [match_mode] argument to specify whether to return the closest match or an exact match, and the optional [search_mode] argument to specify whether to search from the beginning or end of the lookup array.

Step 3: Press **Enter** to execute the formula. Excel will search for the value "101" in the ID column of the employee table and return the corresponding value from the Salary column, which is $60,000.

You can find the salaries of other employees by changing the lookup value in the XLOOKUP formula to the desired ID number.

Note: This is just one example of how to use XLOOKUP and provides a taster of what it does. I have written a whole book on just the XLOOKUP function alone called *Excel Formulas and Functions: The Step by Step Excel Book for Beginners on how to Master Lookup Formulas using the XLOOKUP Function* as it is a very powerful and useful function to learn.

This book is available on Amazon now. For more information or to purchase it, enter the below links to your web browser:

Amazon UK: www.amazon.co.uk/Excel-Formulas-Functions-Beginners-Function/dp/B08F8193G6

Amazon US: www.amazon.com/Excel-Formulas-Functions-Beginners-Function/dp/B08F8193G6

To Summarise

XLOOKUP is a powerful function in Microsoft Excel that allows you to search for a specific value in a table or range and return a corresponding value from another column in the same table or range. It's a very useful tool for tasks such as finding salaries or other relevant information for a particular employee based on their ID. By using the XLOOKUP formula and specifying the lookup value, lookup array, and return array, you can quickly and easily retrieve the data you need. With its flexibility and ease of use, XLOOKUP is a valuable tool for anyone who works with data in Excel.

INDEX Function

What is it?

The INDEX function in Excel is a built-in function that returns the value of a cell within a specified range, based on the row and column numbers provided as arguments. It is commonly used to extract a specific value or a range of values from a larger table or array.

Syntax

=INDEX(array, row_num, [column_num])

Arguments

- **array** (required): This is the range or array of cells from which you want to extract the value. The array can be a single row or column, a range of cells, or an entire table.

- **row_num** (required): This argument specifies the row number of the cell you want to extract. It must be a positive integer that corresponds to the row number within the specified range or array.
- **column_num**: (optional) This argument specifies the column number of the cell you want to extract. It must be a positive integer that corresponds to the column number within the specified range or array.

Example:

Suppose you have a table of sales data for different products, and you want to retrieve the sales data for a particular product in a specific month. Here's the sample data:

◢	A	B	C	D	E	F	G
1							
2		Product	Jan	Feb	Mar	Apr	
3		A	100	150	200	250	
4		B	50	75	100	125	
5		C	75	100	125	150	
6							

To retrieve the sales data for Product B in February, you can use the INDEX function by specifying row and column numbers. Below are the steps to do this:

Step 1: First, select a cell where you want to display the result. In this example I select cell H3.

H3					✕ ✓ _fx_	=INDEX(C3:F5,2,2)		
◢	A	B	C	D	E	F	G	H
1								
2		Product	Jan	Feb	Mar	Apr		
3		A	100	150	200	250		75
4		B	50	75	100	125		
5		C	75	100	125	150		
6								

Step 2: Next, enter the following formula into cell H3 "**=INDEX(C3:F5,2,2)**".

Let's break down this formula:

- The first argument is the range of cells that contains the data you want to retrieve. In this case, it's the range C3:F5.

26

- The second argument is the row number of the cell you want to retrieve within the range. In this example, it's 2, because we want to retrieve the sales data for Product B which is in row 2 of the range C3:F5.

- The third argument is the column number of the cell you want to retrieve within the range. In this example, it's also 2, because we want to retrieve the sales data for February which is in column 2 of the range C3:F5.

Step 3: Press **Enter** to complete the formula. Excel should display the value 75 in cell H3, which is the sales data for Product B in February.

To Summarise

The INDEX function in Excel is a powerful tool for retrieving specific data from a table or range of cells. By specifying the row and column numbers of the cell you want to retrieve, you can quickly and easily extract information from large datasets. The example provided demonstrates how the INDEX function can be used to retrieve sales data for a particular product in a specific month. By following the step-by-step instructions above and understanding the arguments of the function, you can apply this tool to your own data analysis needs. The INDEX function is just one of many functions in Excel that can help streamline data analysis and make working with large datasets more efficient.

MATCH Function

What is it?

The MATCH function is a built-in function in Excel that returns the relative position of a specified value within a range of cells. The function can be used to search for a value within a row or column and return its position or index number.

Syntax

=MATCH(lookup_value, lookup_array, [match_type])

Arguments

- **lookup_value** (required): This is the value that you want to search for in the lookup_array. It can be a number, text, or logical value.

- **lookup_array** (required): This is the range of cells that you want to search in. It can be a single row or column or a range of cells. The lookup_array must be sorted in ascending order for the MATCH function to work correctly.

- **match_type** (optional): This is an optional argument that specifies how the MATCH function should perform the search. It can take one of three values:

  - 1 (or omitted): The function searches for the closest match that is less than or equal to the lookup_value. This is the default value if the match_type argument is omitted.

  - 0: The function searches for an exact match of the lookup_value within the lookup_array.

- -1: The function searches for the closest match that is greater than or equal to the lookup_value.

Example:

Suppose you have a list of names in column B and their corresponding ages in column C, and you want to find the position of a specific name in the list. Below is what the data looks like:

	A	B	C	D
1				
2		Name	Age	
3		John	32	
4		Jane	28	
5		Alice	45	
6		Mark	37	
7		Peter	52	
8		Sarah	24	
9		Matt	42	
10				

To retrieve the position for Jane in the table using the MATCH function, follow the steps below:

Step 1: First, select a cell where you want to display the result. In this example I select cell F2.

| F2 | | | | | ▾ | ⋮ | ✕ | ✓ | f_x | =MATCH(E2,B3:B9,0) |

	A	B	C	D	E	F	G	H
1								
2		Name	Age		Jane	2		
3		John	32					
4		Jane	28					
5		Alice	45					
6		Mark	37					
7		Peter	52					
8		Sarah	24					
9		Matt	42					
10								

Step 2: In the selected cell, enter the following formula "=**MATCH(E2,B3:B9,0)**".

Here is how the formula works:

- Lookup value is E2. This is the value we want to find in the lookup array. In this case, we're searching for the name "Jane".

- Lookup array is B3:B9. This is the range of cells that we want to search for the lookup value. In this case, we're searching for the name "Jane" in the range B3:B9 of the worksheet.

- Match type is 0. This specifies the type of match that we want to perform. A value of 0 means we want to find an exact match for the lookup value. If we had entered 1 instead, Excel would perform an approximate match and return the position of the closest value in the lookup array that is less than or equal to the lookup value. Similarly, if we had entered -1, Excel would perform an approximate match and return the position of the closest value in the lookup array that is greater than or equal to the lookup value.

- Putting all of these arguments together, the MATCH function looks for the value in cell E2 (i.e. "Jane") in the range B3:B9 of the worksheet, and returns the position of the first cell in the lookup array that contains an exact match for that value.

Step 3: Press **Enter** to calculate the formula. The result should be the position of the name you searched for in the list of names. In this case, since "Jane" is in the second row of the range B3:B9, the formula returns the value 2.

Note: If the lookup_value is not found in the lookup_array, the function returns the #N/A error.

To Summarise

The MATCH function is a powerful tool in Microsoft Excel that allows you to find the position of a value within a range of cells. By using this function with a lookup value, lookup array, and match type, you can quickly and easily retrieve the position of a specific value in a table, list, or database. This can be especially useful when working with large datasets or when you need to locate specific information within a worksheet. By following the step-by-step instructions provided above, you can use the MATCH function in your own Excel spreadsheets to search for specific values and retrieve the position of those values within a range of cells.

INDEX-MATCH Functions

What is it?

You have learnt what the INDEX and MATCH functions are and how they work with examples. However, by combining the INDEX and MATCH functions together, you can perform even more powerful lookups. As you have discovered, the INDEX function returns the value of a cell in a table based on its row and column numbers, while the MATCH function searches for a specified value in a range and returns its position.

To use both these functions together to perform a lookup, you can use the MATCH function to find the row or column number of the desired value, and then use the INDEX function to retrieve the value at that position.

Example:

Suppose you have a table of employee data that looks like this:

	A	B	C	D	E
1					
2		Employee Name	Employee ID	Department	
3		John Smith	12345	Sales	
4		Jane Doe	23456	Marketing	
5		Bob Johnson	34567	IT	
6		Sarah Lee	45678	HR	
7					

You want to use the Employee ID in column C to look up the corresponding Department in column D. In this example, I want to return the Department for Employee ID 23456. Here are the steps to do this by combining the INDEX and MATCH functions together:

Step 1: Select a cell where you want to display the result of the lookup. In this example, I select cell G3.

G3   *fx*   =INDEX(D3:D6,MATCH(F3,C3:C6,0))

	A	B	C	D	E	F	G	H
1								
2		Employee Name	Employee ID	Department				
3		John Smith	12345	Sales		23456	Marketing	
4		Jane Doe	23456	Marketing				
5		Bob Johnson	34567	IT				
6		Sarah Lee	45678	HR				
7								

Step 2: In that cell, type the following formula "=**INDEX(D3:D6,MATCH(F3,C3:C6,0))**".

Here is how the formula works:

- The MATCH function looks for the value in cell F3 (the Employee ID) within the C3:C6 range (the Employee ID column), and returns the row number where it finds a match. The 0 at the end of the MATCH function tells Excel to look for an exact match.

- The INDEX function takes the row number returned by MATCH and uses it to look up the corresponding value in the D3:D6 range (the Department column).

Let's break this formula a bit further to see exactly what's happening:

- MATCH(F3,C3:C6,0) finds the row number where the Employee ID in cell F3 appears in column C.

- The result of MATCH is then passed as the row number argument to INDEX.

- INDEX(D3:D6, row number) returns the value in the same row of column D.

- So in this case, the formula is saying "find the row number where the Employee ID in cell F3, i.e. "23456" appears in column C, then return the corresponding value in column D in that same row".

Step 3: Press **Enter** to execute the formula. The result should be the Department associated with the Employee ID you looked up. In this case, if you looked up Employee ID 23456, the result should be "Marketing".

The example above shows you how to perform a row lookup. Here is another example of how to combine the INDEX and MATCH functions to create a more powerful formula by looking up both the row and column position of an array.

Let's say we have a table that shows the scores of different students in different subjects:

	A	B	C	D	E	F
1						
2		Student Name	Math	Science	English	
3		John	90	80	95	
4		Sarah	85	90	92	
5		Mike	92	88	87	
6		Emily	80	85	90	
7						

We want to find the scores of a specific student, let's say Sarah for Science. We can use the following steps to do this:

Step 1: Start by selecting a cell where we want the result to be displayed. In this example, I will use cell H5.

H5 f_x =INDEX(C3:E6,MATCH(H3,B3:B6,0),MATCH(H4,C2:E2,0))

	A	B	C	D	E	F	G	H	I	J	K
1											
2		Student Name	Math	Science	English						
3		John	90	80	95		Name:	Sarah			
4		Sarah	85	90	92		Subject:	Science			
5		Mike	92	88	87		Grade:	90			
6		Emily	80	85	90						
7											
8											
9											

Step 2: Type the following formula "**=INDEX(C3:E6,MATCH(H3,B3:B6,0),MATCH(H4,C2:E2,0))**".

Let's break this formula down:

- The first MATCH function finds the row position for Sarah. It looks for the value in cell H3 (the Student Name) within the B3:B6 range (the Student Name column), and returns the row number where it finds a match. The 0 at the end of the MATCH function tells Excel to look for an exact match.

- The second MATCH function finds the column position for the subject Science. It looks for the value in cell H4 (the Subject) within the C2:E2 range (the Subject columns), and returns the column number where it finds a match. The 0 at the end of the MATCH function tells Excel to look for an exact match.

- The INDEX function takes the row number returned by the first MATCH and uses it to look up the corresponding value in the B3:B6 range (the Student Name column). It then takes the column number

31

returned by the second MATCH and uses it to look up the corresponding value in the C2:E2 range (the Subject columns).

Step 3: Press **Enter** to calculate the formula. The result should return 90.

To Summarise

The combination of INDEX and MATCH functions in Excel is a powerful tool that allows users to perform lookups and retrieve data from tables. This function is useful when searching for specific data in large datasets or when you need to retrieve a row or column of data based on a specific value. By using the MATCH function to find the position of the data in the table and the INDEX function to retrieve the data, users can perform complex lookups with ease. This function is a great addition to the Excel toolset and can help users save time and increase their productivity.

XMATCH Function

What is it?

The XMATCH function is a new and improved version of the MATCH function in Microsoft Excel, which allows for more flexibility and power when searching for values in a range or array. The XMATCH function was introduced in Excel 365, so it may not be available in earlier versions of Excel.

Syntax

=XMATCH(lookup_value, lookup_array, [match_mode], [search_mode])

Arguments

- **lookup_value** (required): This is the value you want to search for in the lookup_array.

- **lookup_array** (required): This is the range or array of cells in which you want to search for the lookup_value.

- **match_mode** (optional): This argument specifies whether the lookup should be an exact match or an approximate match. It can take one of three values:

  - 0 or omitted: This is the default value, and it performs an exact match.

  - 1: This specifies an approximate match using the "closest match" rule. The lookup_array must be sorted in ascending order.

  - -1: This specifies an approximate match using the "closest match" rule. The lookup_array must be sorted in descending order.

- **search_mode** (optional): This argument specifies the type of search to perform. It can take one of three values:

  - 1 or omitted: This is the default value, and it performs a binary search.

- 2: This specifies a linear search.

- -1: This specifies a binary search, but the lookup_array must be sorted in descending order.

Example:

Suppose you have the following data in cells B2:C7:

	A	B	C	D
1				
2		Item	Quantity	
3		Apple	10	
4		Banana	20	
5		Cherry	15	
6		Grape	25	
7		Mango	30	
8				

You want to find the position of Cherry in the Item column. Here are the steps to do this using the XMATCH function:

Step 1: Click on an empty cell where you want to display the result. In this example, I select cell F3.

F3				✕ ✓ *fx*	=XMATCH(E3,B3:B7,0)		

	A	B	C	D	E	F	G	H
1								
2		Item	Quantity					
3		Apple	10		Cherry	3		
4		Banana	20					
5		Cherry	15					
6		Grape	25					
7		Mango	30					
8								

Step 2: Type the XMATCH formula "**=XMATCH(E3,B3:B7,0)**" in the selected cell.

Below is a breakdown of the formula:

- "Cherry" in cell E3 is the lookup value and the value you want to match.

- B3:B7 is the lookup array where you want to search for the value.

- The match mode is 0 which indicates that you want an exact match.

- So the formula tells Excel to search the range B3:B7 for the value "Cherry", and return the position of the cell where it's found.

Step 3: Press **Enter** to execute the formula. The result will be 3 because Cherry is in the 3rd row of the Item column.

Note: The XMATCH function is an improvement over the MATCH function because it offers more options for searching and matching values. With the XMATCH function, you can perform approximate matches using either a binary or linear search, and you can also specify whether the lookup_array is sorted in ascending or descending order.

To Summarise

Overall, the XMATCH function is a powerful tool for searching and matching values in Excel, and it can be very useful for a wide range of applications, including data analysis, financial modelling, and more.

LOOKUP Function

What is it?

The Excel LOOKUP function is used to search for a value in a sorted array or range, and then returns the corresponding value in a specified column or row. This function is useful when you need to find a specific value in a large set of data.

Syntax

=LOOKUP(lookup_value, lookup_vector, [result_vector])

Arguments

- **lookup_value** (required): This is the value you are looking for in the lookup_vector. It can be a value, reference, or cell.

- **lookup_vector** (required): This is the range of cells or array where the lookup_value is located. The lookup_vector must be sorted in ascending order, otherwise, the result may be incorrect.

- **result_vector**: (optional) This is the range of cells or array where the corresponding value is located. If the result_vector is not provided, the lookup_vector will be used as the result_vector.

Example:

Suppose we have a table of data that shows the letter grades corresponding to different numerical scores as shown below:

	A	B	C	D	E
1	Score	Grade			
2	0	F		Score:	85
3	60	D		Grade:	
4	70	C			
5	80	B			
6	90	A			
7					

We want to use the LOOKUP function to find the letter grade for a given score, let's say 85. We will insert the letter grade for the score in cell E3. Below are the steps to do this:

Step 1: First, select a cell where you want to display the result. In this example, I select cell E3.

E3			✕ ✓ f_x	=LOOKUP(E2,A2:A6,B2:B6)				
	A	B	C	D	E	F	G	H
1	Score	Grade						
2	0	F		Score:	85			
3	60	D		Grade:	B			
4	70	C						
5	80	B						
6	90	A						
7								

Step 2: Next, enter the following formula into cell E3 "**=LOOKUP(E2,A2:A6,B2:B6)**".

Let's break down this formula:

- Cell E2 is the lookup_value argument, which is the score that we want to find the letter grade for.

- Range A2:A6 is the lookup_vector argument, which is the range of scores that the grades are associated with.

- Range B2:B6 is the result_vector argument, which is the range of letter grades corresponding to the scores.

- The LOOKUP function searches for the lookup_value argument (which is 85 in this example) in the lookup_vector argument, and then returns the corresponding value from the result_vector argument. Since 85 falls between 80 and 90 in the lookup_vector, the function returns the corresponding value from the result_vector, which is "B".

Step 3: Press **Enter** to complete the formula. Excel should return the letter grade "B".

Note: The lookup_vector must be sorted in ascending order for the function to work properly. If it is not sorted, the function may return incorrect results.

To Summarise

Overall, the LOOKUP function can be a valuable tool for anyone working with Excel who needs to search for values within a large dataset. With a basic understanding of the syntax and how the function works, users can quickly and easily find the information they need without having to manually search through large amounts of data.

Logical Functions

Excel logical functions return either a TRUE or FALSE value based on a logical test or comparison. They are commonly used in Excel formulas and conditional formatting to automate decision-making processes. By using Excel logical functions, users can perform powerful calculations and make informed decisions based on data. In this chapter we will explore the most commonly used logical functions.

IF Function

What is it?

The IF function is a conditional function in Microsoft Excel that allows you to perform different actions based on a logical test. The function evaluates a specified condition and returns one value if the condition is true, and another value if the condition is false.

Syntax

=IF(logical_test, value_if_true, value_if_false)

Arguments

- **logical_test** (required): This is a required argument that specifies the condition to be tested. It can be a logical expression, a cell reference, or a value. If the logical_test is true, the function returns the value_if_true argument; otherwise, it returns the value_if_false argument.

- **value_if_true** (required): This is the value that the function returns if the logical_test argument is true. It can be a value, a formula, or a cell reference.

- **value_if_false** (optional): This is the value that the function returns if the logical_test argument is false. It can be a value, a formula, or a cell reference.

Example 1:

Suppose you have a list of exam scores and you want to check which students scored above 80. Here is what the data looks like:

	A	B	C	D
1				
2		Exam Scores	Above 80	
3		75		
4		90		
5		85		
6		60		
7		80		
8		95		
9				

The goal is to enter an IF formula in column C which returns a "Yes" if the score is above 80 and "No" if it is below 80. Here are the steps to do this:

C3		▼	:	✕	✓	fx	=IF(B3>80, "Yes", "No")		
	A	B		C		D	E	F	G
1									
2		Exam Scores		Above 80					
3		75		No					
4		90							
5		85							
6		60							
7		80							
8		95							
9									

Step 1: In the first cell in C3 in the Above 80 column, type the following formula "**=IF(B3>80, "Yes", "No")**".

Here is how the formula works:

- Cell B3 is used as the logical_test argument and will check if the exam score is greater than 80.

- If it is, the value_if_true argument will display "Yes" in the Above 80 column.

- If it isn't above 80, the value_if_false argument will display "No".

Step 2: Press **Enter**.

C3		▼	:	✕	✓	fx	=IF(B3>80, "Yes", "No")		
	A	B		C		D	E	F	G
1									
2		Exam Scores		Above 80					
3		75		No					
4		90		Yes					
5		85		Yes					
6		60		No					
7		80		No					
8		95		Yes					
9									

Step 3: Copy the formula down to the rest of the cells in column C in the Above 80 column. The cells will display a "Yes" if any score in column B is over 80 and "No" if it is below 80.

Example 2:

This next example will use the IF function to calculate a bonus amount based on sales performance.

	A	B	C	D	E
1					
2		Salesperson	Sales Figures	Bonus	
3		John	12000		
4		Sarah	8000		
5		Mark	15000		
6		Jane	6000		
7		Tom	11000		
8					

Suppose you have a list of salespeople in column B and their sales figures in column C, and you want to calculate a bonus amount based on their performance. If the salespersons sales figure is above 10,000, then you give a 10% bonus otherwise there is no bonus. You can use the IF function to do this.

D3					✕ ✓ f_x	=IF(C3>10000, C3*0.1, 0)		
	A	B	C	D	E	F	G	
1								
2		Salesperson	Sales Figures	Bonus				
3		John	12000	1200				
4		Sarah	8000					
5		Mark	15000					
6		Jane	6000					
7		Tom	11000					
8								

Step 1: In the first cell of the Bonus column, type the following formula "**=IF(C3>10000, C3*0.1, 0)**".

Here is how the formula works:

- Cell C3 is used as the logical_test argument and will check if the sales figure is greater than 10000.

- If it is greater than 10000, the value_if_true argument will multiply the sales figure in cell C3 by 0.1.

- If it isn't above 10000, the value_if_false argument will display a zero.

Step 2: Press **Enter** to calculate the result.

D3					✕ ✓ f_x	=IF(C3>10000, C3*0.1, 0)		
	A	B	C	D	E	F	G	
1								
2		Salesperson	Sales Figures	Bonus				
3		John	12000	1200				
4		Sarah	8000	0				
5		Mark	15000	1500				
6		Jane	6000	0				
7		Tom	11000	1100				
8								

Step 3: Copy the formula down to the rest of the cells in the Bonus column. The formula will calculate a bonus of 10% for all salespeople with sales above 10,000. The bonus will be allocated to "John", "Mark" and "Tom".

Example 3:

You can also nest IF functions to create more logical formulas.

	A	B	C	D	E	F
1						
2		Salesperson	Product Type	Sales Figures	Commission	
3		John	Product A	12000		
4		Sarah	Product B	8000		
5		Mark	Product A	15000		
6		Jane	Product B	6000		
7		Tom	Product C	11000		
8						

Suppose you have a list of sales figures and you want to calculate a commission rate based on the salesperson's performance and the type of product they sold. You can use the IF function with nested conditions to do this. Here are the steps to do this:

E3   fx   =IF(D3>10000, IF(C3="Product A", 0.15, 0.1), IF(C3="Product A", 0.1, 0.05))

	A	B	C	D	E	F	G	H	I	J	K
1											
2		Salesperson	Product Type	Sales Figures	Commission						
3		John	Product A	12000	0.15						
4		Sarah	Product B	8000							
5		Mark	Product A	15000							
6		Jane	Product B	6000							
7		Tom	Product C	11000							
8											

Step 1: In the first cell of the Commission column, type the following formula "**=IF(D3>10000, IF(C3="Product A", 0.15, 0.1), IF(C3="Product A", 0.1, 0.05))**".

Here is how the formula works:

- The formula will first check if the sales figure in cell D3 is greater than 10000. If it is, it will check if the product type in cell C3 is "Product A". If it is, it will calculate a commission rate of 15%. If it isn't, it will calculate a commission rate of 10%.

- If the sales figure in cell D3 is not greater than 10000, the formula will check if the product type in cell C3 is "Product A". If it is, it will calculate a commission rate of 10%. If it isn't, it will calculate a commission rate of 5%.

Step 2: Press **Enter** to calculate the result.

E3				f_x	=IF(D3>10000, IF(C3="Product A", 0.15, 0.1), IF(C3="Product A", 0.1, 0.05))					

	A	B	C	D	E	F	G	H	I	J	K
1											
2		Salesperson	Product Type	Sales Figures	Commission						
3		John	Product A	12000	0.15						
4		Sarah	Product B	8000	0.05						
5		Mark	Product A	15000	0.15						
6		Jane	Product B	6000	0.05						
7		Tom	Product C	11000	0.1						
8											

Step 3: Copy the formula down to the rest of the cells in the Commission column.

Note: The logical_test argument can be any logical expression that returns TRUE or FALSE. For example, you can use comparison operators such as >, <, >=, <=, =, or <>, as well as logical operators such as AND, OR, or NOT.

To Summarise

The IF function is a powerful tool in Microsoft Excel that allows users to automate decision-making processes based on specific conditions. It can be used to perform simple tasks like checking if a value meets a certain criteria, or more complex tasks like calculating commission rates based on multiple conditions. By following the step-by-step instructions and examples provided above, users can gain a better understanding of how to use the IF function effectively in their spreadsheets. With its versatility and usefulness, the IF function is a valuable tool for anyone working with data in Excel.

AND Function

What is it?

The AND function is a logical function in Excel that returns TRUE if all the arguments provided to it are TRUE, and FALSE if any of the arguments are FALSE. It is commonly used in combination with other logical functions to evaluate complex conditions in Excel.

Syntax

=AND(logical1, [logical2], ...)

Arguments

- **logical1** (required): This is the first condition to be evaluated. It can be a logical expression or a reference to a cell containing a logical value. If the value of logical1 is TRUE, the function moves on to evaluate the next logical argument (if any); otherwise, the function returns FALSE.

- **logical2, logical3, ...** (optional): These are additional conditions to be evaluated. You can include up to 255 logical arguments. Each argument can be a logical expression or a reference to a cell containing a logical value. If all the arguments are TRUE, the function returns TRUE; otherwise, it returns FALSE.

Example:

Suppose we have a table of sales data for different products, and we want to identify the products that sold more than 100 units in both Q1 and Q2 and then display the results in column E. Here is what the data looks like:

	A	B	C	D	E	F
1						
2		Product	Q1 Sales	Q2 Sales	Q1 and Q2 Sales	
3		A	120	80		
4		B	90	110		
5		C	150	130		
6		D	80	120		
7						

Below are the steps to do this using the AND function:

E3   ✕ ✓ *fx*   =AND(C3>100,D3>100)

	A	B	C	D	E	F	G
1							
2		Product	Q1 Sales	Q2 Sales	Q1 and Q2 Sales		
3		A	120	80	FALSE		
4		B	90	110			
5		C	150	130			
6		D	80	120			
7							

Step 1: In cell E3, enter the formula "**=AND(C3>100,D3>100)**".

Here is a breakdown of the formula:

- C3>100: This is the first condition being tested. It checks if the sales in Q1 for Product A is greater than 100.

- D3>100: This is the second condition being tested. It checks if the sales in Q2 for Product A is greater than 100.

- The AND function then checks whether both of the conditions are true.

- If just one or no conditions are true, the AND function returns FALSE, indicating that Product A does not meet both criteria (Q1 sales greater than 100 and Q2 sales greater than 100). If both conditions are TRUE, the AND function returns TRUE, indicating that Product A meets both of the criteria.

Step 2: Press **Enter** to calculate the result.

	A	B	C	D	E	F	G
1							
2		Product	Q1 Sales	Q2 Sales	Q1 and Q2 Sales		
3		A	120	80	FALSE		
4		B	90	110	FALSE		
5		C	150	130	TRUE		
6		D	80	120	FALSE		
7							

E3 — `=AND(C3>100,D3>100)`

Step 3: Copy the formula down to the other rows in the table. The result in each row will be either TRUE or FALSE, depending on whether the product sold more than 100 units in both Q1 and Q2. In the example above, the AND function in cells E3, E4 and E6 returns FALSE because products A, B and D did not sell more than 100 units in both Q1 and Q2. The AND function in cell E5 returns TRUE because product C sold more than 100 units in both Q1 and Q2.

To Summarise

The AND function in Excel is a logical function that allows you to test multiple conditions and return a TRUE or FALSE result based on whether all the conditions are met. The function takes one or more arguments that can be either logical values (TRUE or FALSE), expressions that evaluate to logical values, or cell references that contain logical values. When all the arguments evaluate to TRUE, the function returns TRUE; otherwise, it returns FALSE. The AND function is a powerful tool that can be used in a variety of scenarios, such as checking if two conditions are both true or testing if multiple conditions are met before taking a certain action. By understanding how to use the AND function in Excel, you can save time and streamline your spreadsheet calculations.

OR Function

What is it?

The Excel OR function is a logical function that returns a TRUE or FALSE value based on whether any of the supplied conditions are true or not.

Syntax

=OR(logical1, [logical2], ...)

Arguments

- **logical1** (required): The first condition to evaluate. This argument can be a value, expression, or cell reference that evaluates to either TRUE or FALSE.

- **logical2** (optional): Additional conditions to evaluate. You can specify up to 255 conditions separated by commas. Each additional condition is evaluated in the same way as logical1.

Example:

Suppose we have a list of employees and their salaries in an Excel sheet, and we want to find out which employees are either earning a salary greater than $100,000 or have worked for the company for more than 5 years. Here is what the data looks like:

	A	B	C	D	E	F
1						
2		Employee	Salary (USD)	Years	Result	
3		1	120000	6		
4		2	90000	2		
5		3	110000	4		
6		4	95000	7		
7		5	130000	3		
8						

In column E, we want to put an OR formula in to return a TRUE or FALSE value. Here are the steps to do this:

E3   ▼   ⋮   ✕   ✓   *fx*   =OR(C3>100000, D3>5)

	A	B	C	D	E	F
1						
2		Employee	Salary (USD)	Years	Result	
3		1	120000	6	TRUE	
4		2	90000	2		
5		3	110000	4		
6		4	95000	7		
7		5	130000	3		
8						

Step 1: In cell E3, enter the formula "**=OR(C3>100000, D3>5)**".

Here is how each part of the formula works:

- C3>100000: This is the first condition being tested. It checks if the salary in cell C3 is greater than $100,000.

- D3>5: This is the second condition being tested. It checks if the number of years the employee has worked in cell D3 is greater than 5.

- The OR function then checks whether at least one of the conditions is true.

- If either condition is true for a given employee, the OR function returns TRUE, indicating that the employee meets at least one of the criteria (salary greater than $100,000 or has worked for more than 5 years). If both conditions are false for a given employee, the OR function returns FALSE, indicating that the employee does not meet either of the criteria.

Step 2: Press **Enter** to calculate the result.

	A	B	C	D	E	F
1						
2		Employee	Salary (USD)	Years	Result	
3		1	120000	6	TRUE	
4		2	90000	2	FALSE	
5		3	110000	4	TRUE	
6		4	95000	7	TRUE	
7		5	130000	3	TRUE	
8						

E3 : fx =OR(C3>100000, D3>5)

Step 3: Copy the formula down to the other rows in the table. In this example, the OR function returns TRUE for employees 1, 3, 4 and 5 because they either earn a salary greater than $100,000 or have worked for the company for more than 5 years. The function returns FALSE for employees 2 because neither condition is true.

To Summarise

The OR function in Excel is a powerful tool that allows users to test multiple conditions at once and return a single result. By using the OR function, users can easily evaluate complex data sets and make informed decisions based on the results. With the step-by-step instructions provided above and the example data, you should be able to apply the OR function in your own Excel worksheets and analyse the data more efficiently.

IFS Function

What is it?

The IFS function in Microsoft Excel is a logical function that allows you to test multiple conditions and return a value based on the first true condition. It replaces the need for nested IF statements, making complex logical tests easier to write and read.

Syntax

=IFS(logical_test1, value_if_true1, [logical_test2, value_if_true2], …)

Arguments

- **logical_test1** (required): This is the first logical expression that you want to test. It can be any expression that returns a logical value (TRUE or FALSE).

- **value_if_true1** (required): This is the value that will be returned if the first logical_test1 is TRUE.

- **logical_test2, value_if_true2** (optional): These are additional logical expressions and values that you want to test. You can include up to 127 additional pairs of logical expressions and values. Each pair must be enclosed in square brackets and separated by a comma.

Example:

Suppose you have a dataset that contains the names of different fruits and their corresponding prices, and you want to categorise the fruits based on their prices into three categories: "Expensive", "Moderate", and "Cheap". Below is what the data set looks like:

	A	B	C	D	E
1					
2		Fruit	Price	Category	
3		Apple	1.5		
4		Banana	2.25		
5		Orange	3.75		
6		Mango	5.5		
7		Grape	0.75		
8					

The price equal to 5 or above is classed as expensive. A price equal or above 2 is classed as moderate and anything below 2 is cheap. We want to enter the results in column D. Here's how you can use the Excel IFS function to categorise the fruits based on their prices:

D3 f_x =IFS(C3>=5,"Expensive",C3>=2,"Moderate",C3<2,"Cheap")

	A	B	C	D	E	F	G	H	I	J
1										
2		Fruit	Price	Category						
3		Apple	1.5	Cheap						
4		Banana	2.25							
5		Orange	3.75							
6		Mango	5.5							
7		Grape	0.75							
8										

Step 1: In cell D3, enter the formula "**=IFS(C3>=5,"Expensive",C3>=2,"Moderate",C3<2,"Cheap")**".

Here's how the formula works:

- The first condition is C3>=5, which checks whether the price in cell C3 is greater than or equal to 5. If this condition is met, the formula returns "Expensive".

- If the first condition is not met, the formula moves on to the next condition, which is C3>=2. This condition checks whether the price in cell C3 is greater than or equal to 2. If this condition is met, the formula returns "Moderate".

- If neither of the first two conditions are met, the formula moves on to the final condition, which is C3<2. This condition checks whether the price in cell C3 is less than 2. If this condition is met, the formula returns "Cheap".

- So, in short, the IFS function checks the price of each fruit in the dataset and assigns it to one of three categories based on its price. If the price is greater than or equal to 5, it's categorised as "Expensive". If it's greater than or equal to 2 but less than 5, it's categorised as "Moderate". If it's less than 2, it's categorised as "Cheap".

Step 2: Press **Enter** to apply the function to the first cell. The result should show the category of the fruit based on its price.

D3				fx	=IFS(C3>=5,"Expensive",C3>=2,"Moderate",C3<2,"Cheap")					
	A	B	C	D	E	F	G	H	I	J
1										
2		Fruit	Price	Category						
3		Apple	1.5	Cheap						
4		Banana	2.25	Moderate						
5		Orange	3.75	Moderate						
6		Mango	5.5	Expensive						
7		Grape	0.75	Cheap						
8										

Step 3: Copy the formula from the first cell to the rest of the cells in the Category column. Each fruit is now categorised based on its price.

To Summarise

The IFS function in Excel is a powerful tool that allows you to categorise data based on multiple conditions. By using the IFS function, you can quickly and easily categorise data into different groups, making it easier to analyse and make decisions based on the data. In the example provided, we saw how the IFS function was used to categorise fruits based on their prices into three categories: "Expensive", "Moderate", and "Cheap". By following the steps provided, you can use the IFS function to categorise your own data based on the conditions that are important to you.

IFERROR Function

What is it?

The IFERROR function in Excel is a formula that allows you to handle errors in a more organised and efficient way. It is typically used in situations where a formula might return an error, such as a #VALUE! or #DIV/0! error, and you want to display a specific value or message instead of the error.

Syntax

=IFERROR(value, value_if_error)

Arguments

- **value** (required): This is the expression or formula that you want to evaluate. If this value results in an error, the IFERROR function will return the value specified in the second argument (value_if_error).

- **value_if_error** (required): This is the value or message that you want to return if the first argument results in an error.

Example:

Below shows sample data in columns A and B.

	A	B	C
1	10	5	
2	20	0	
3	30	#DIV/0!	
4	40	15	
5	50	#VALUE!	
6			

The goal is to divide the figures in column A by column B and to return an "Error" message if there is an error in the calculation. To do this, we need to enter an IFERROR formula in column C. Here are the steps to do this:

C1			× ✓ f_x	=IFERROR(A1/B1, "Error")				
	A	B	C	D	E	F	G	
1	10	5	2					
2	20	0						
3	30	#DIV/0!						
4	40	15						
5	50	#VALUE!						
6								

Step 1: In cell C1, enter the following formula "**=IFERROR(A1/B1, "Error")**".

Here is how the formula works:

- This formula divides the value in cell A1 by the value in cell B1.

- If this calculation produces a valid result, the result is displayed in cell C1.

- However, if there is an error in the calculation (such as dividing by zero or a non-numeric value), the IFERROR function returns the text "Error" instead of the error message.

Step 2: Press **Enter**, and you should see the result 2 in cell C1, which is the result of dividing 10 by 5.

C1			× ✓ f_x	=IFERROR(A1/B1, "Error")				
	A	B	C	D	E	F	G	H
1	10	5	2					
2	20	0	Error					
3	30	#DIV/0!	Error					
4	40	15	2.666666667					
5	50	#VALUE!	Error					
6								

Step 3: Copy the formula from cell C1 and paste it into cells C2 to C5.

In this example, the IFERROR function helps to handle any errors that may occur in the division calculation. If there is an error, it returns the text "Error" instead of the error message, making the spreadsheet more readable and easier to understand.

To Summarise

The Excel IFERROR function is a useful tool that allows users to handle errors that may occur in their calculations. By using this function, users can specify what value to display when an error occurs, rather than seeing the error message in the cell. This not only makes the spreadsheet more organised and readable but also helps to avoid confusion and mistakes that could occur when dealing with error messages. Overall, the IFERROR function is a simple yet powerful tool that makes your worksheets look more clean and presentable.

Text Functions

Excel text functions are a group of built-in functions that are designed to manipulate and analyse text strings in Microsoft Excel. These functions are useful when you need to extract, combine, format, or analyse text data in your worksheets.

LEFT Function

What is it?

The Excel LEFT function is a text function that allows you to extract a specified number of characters from the left side of a text string. This function is useful when you need to extract a specific part of a longer string of text, such as a name or a code, and use it elsewhere in your spreadsheet.

Syntax

=LEFT(text, [num_chars])

Arguments

- **text** (required): This is the text string that you want to extract characters from. It can be a cell reference, a text string in quotation marks, or the result of another formula.

- **num_chars** (optional): This is the number of characters that you want to extract from the left side of the text string. If you omit this argument, the function will extract one character by default. If you specify a value for this argument that is greater than the total number of characters in the text string, the function will return the entire text string.

Example:

Suppose you have a list of names in column A, and you want to extract the first three characters of each name into column B using the LEFT function. The sample data looks like this:

	A	B
1	Name	
2	John Doe	
3	Jane Smith	
4	James Johnson	
5	Sarah Lee	
6		

Follow the steps below to extract the first three characters of the first name:

B2		▾	⋮	✕	✓	*fx*	=LEFT(A2,3)	

◢	A	B	C	D
1	Name	Extract First 3 Characters		
2	John Doe	Joh		
3	Jane Smith			
4	James Johnson			
5	Sarah Lee			
6				

Step 1: In cell B2, enter the LEFT function and specify the cell you want to extract the characters from (in this case, A2), and the number of characters you want to extract (in this case, 3). The formula will be "**=LEFT(A2,3)**".

This is a breakdown of the formula:

- The first argument of the LEFT function is the text string to extract characters from, which is cell A2 in this case.

- The second argument is the number of characters to extract from the left of the text string, which is 3.

Step 2: Press **Enter** to complete the formula. The result should be the first three characters of the name in cell A2, which in this case is "Joh".

B2		▾	⋮	✕	✓	*fx*	=LEFT(A2,3)	

◢	A	B	C	D
1	Name	Extract First 3 Characters		
2	John Doe	Joh		
3	Jane Smith	Jan		
4	James Johnson	Jam		
5	Sarah Lee	Sar		
6				

Step 3: Copy the formula down to the other cells in column B. Once you've copied the formula to all the cells in column B, the result should be the first three characters of each name in column A.

To change the number of characters you want to extract from the left, just change the value in the num_chars argument. For example, if you want to extract 4 characters from the left, just change the value to 4.

To Summarise

The Excel LEFT function is a powerful tool that allows you to extract a specific number of characters from the left side of a text string. With this function, you can easily extract and manipulate data in your spreadsheet, making it more useful and relevant to your needs. By providing the text string and the number of characters to extract, you can quickly obtain the desired information from a larger text string. This can be particularly useful in situations where you need to extract names, codes, or other information from a larger dataset. With its simple syntax and easy-to-use arguments, the LEFT function is a valuable tool for any Excel user who needs to work with text strings in their spreadsheets.

RIGHT Function

What is it?

The Excel RIGHT function is a built-in text function that allows users to extract a specified number of characters from the right end of a text string. For example, if you have a list of product codes and you want to extract the last two digits to identify the product type, you can use the RIGHT function to extract those characters.

Syntax

=RIGHT(text,[num_chars])

Arguments

- **text** (required): This is the text string that you want to extract characters from. It can be entered directly into the formula or referenced from a cell.

- **num_chars** (optional): This argument specifies the number of characters that you want to extract from the right end of the text string. If this argument is omitted, the function will extract one character by default.

Example:

Suppose we have the following data in an Excel spreadsheet which shows a list of product names in column B and the SKU's in column C:

	A	B	C	D
1				
2		Product Name	SKU	
3		T-Shirt XL Red	TS-10	
4		Polo Shirt M Blue	PS-20	
5		Hoodie L Black	HD-30	
6		Tank Top S White	TT-40	
7				

We want to extract the last two characters of the SKU number for each product. Here's how we can do this using the RIGHT function:

D3		▼	⋮	✕ ✓	f_x	=RIGHT(C3,2)	

◢	A	B	C	D	E
1					
2		**Product Name**	**SKU**	**SKU Last 2**	
3		T-Shirt XL Red	TS-10	10	
4		Polo Shirt M Blue	PS-20		
5		Hoodie L Black	HD-30		
6		Tank Top S White	TT-40		
7					

Step 1: In cell D3, enter the formula "=**RIGHT(C3,2)**".

Here is how the formula works:

- C3 is the text argument. This tells Excel to extract characters from the SKU number in cell C3.

- 2 is the num_chars argument. This tells Excel to extract the last two characters from the SKU number in cell C3.

Step 2: Press **Enter** to complete the formula for the first row. The result should be the last two characters of the SKU in cell C3, which in this case is 10.

D3		▼	⋮	✕ ✓	f_x	=RIGHT(C3,2)	

◢	A	B	C	D	E
1					
2		**Product Name**	**SKU**	**SKU Last 2**	
3		T-Shirt XL Red	TS-10	10	
4		Polo Shirt M Blue	PS-20	20	
5		Hoodie L Black	HD-30	30	
6		Tank Top S White	TT-40	40	
7					

Step 3: Copy the formula down to the other cells in column D. Once you've copied the formula down in the column, the result returns the last two characters of each SKU in column C.

To change the number of characters you want to extract from the right, just change the value in the num_chars argument. For example, if you want to extract 3 characters from the right, just change the value to 3.

To Summarise

The RIGHT function in Excel is a useful tool for extracting a specified number of characters from the right-hand side of a string. By following the step-by-step instructions above, we were able to use the RIGHT function to extract the last two characters of the SKU number for each product in our example data set. The result was a new column that displayed the extracted characters, which can be used for further analysis or sorting purposes.

MID Function

What is it?

The Excel MID function allows users to extract a specific number of characters from a text string, starting at a specified position. The function stands for "middle" since it can be used to extract a portion of text from the middle of a longer string. To use the MID function, you need to provide a text string, a starting position, and the number of characters to extract.

Syntax

=MID(text, start_num, num_chars)

Arguments

- **text** (required): The text string that contains the substring you want to extract. This can be entered directly into the formula or can be referenced from a cell.

- **start_num** (required): The starting position of the substring you want to extract. This is the position within the text string where the extraction should begin.

- **num_chars** (required): The number of characters to extract from the text string, starting from the position specified in start_num.

Example:

Suppose you have a list of names in column A. The goal is to extract three characters after the second character in each name into column B using the MID function. The sample data looks like this:

	A	B
1	Name	
2	Jonathon	
3	Elizabeth	
4	Samantha	
5	Michael	
6		

Here's how we can do this using the MID function:

B2 f_x =MID(A2,2,3)

	A	B	C	D	E
1	Name	Extract 3 Characters			
2	Jonathon	ona			
3	Elizabeth				
4	Samantha				
5	Michael				
6					

54

Step 1: In cell B2, enter the formula "**=MID(A2,2,3)**".

Here is how the formula works:

- The text argument is the name in cell A2.

- The start_num argument is 2, because we want to start extracting characters from the second position in the name.

- The num_chars argument is 3, because we want to extract the first three characters after the second position of the name.

Step 2: Press **Enter** to complete the formula.

B2	▼	⋮	✕	✓	*fx*	=MID(A2,2,3)	

◢	A	B	C	D	E
1	Name	Extract 3 Characters			
2	Jonathon	ona			
3	Elizabeth	liz			
4	Samantha	ama			
5	Michael	ich			
6					

Step 3: Copy the formula down to the other cells in column B. The MID function has extracted the first three letters of each name after the second character and displayed them in column B.

Note: The MID function can be used to extract both text and numbers from a string.

To Summarise

The MID function in Excel is a powerful tool for extracting specific characters from a text string. By specifying the starting position and number of characters to extract, you can quickly and easily manipulate data in your spreadsheets to meet your needs. With the step-by-step instructions and example provided earlier, you should be able to use the MID function to extract data from your own spreadsheets with ease.

LEN Function

What is it?

The Excel LEN function is a text function that returns the number of characters in a given text string. It can be used to count the number of characters in a cell or a range of cells. It includes spaces and any other non-printable characters. It is useful when you want to count the number of characters in a cell or verify if a text string meets certain length criteria.

Syntax

=LEN(text)

Arguments

- **text** (required): Specifies the text string that you want to count the number of characters. It can be a cell reference, a text string enclosed in quotation marks, or a combination of both.

Example:

Suppose we have a list of names in column A of an Excel spreadsheet, and we want to find out the length of each name and enter it in column B.

	A	B
1	Name	
2	John	
3	Jane	
4	Imran	
5	Kuldeep	
6	Michael	
7	Christopher	
8		

Here's how we can do this using the LEN function:

B2 | ✕ ✓ *fx*   =LEN(A2)

	A	B	C	D	E	F
1	Name	Length				
2	John	4				
3	Jane					
4	Imran					
5	Kuldeep					
6	Michael					
7	Christopher					
8						

Step 1: In cell B2, enter the formula "**=LEN(A2)**".

Here is how the formula works:

- The LEN function takes one argument, which is the text string that you want to find the length of. In this case, we are using cell A2 as the argument, which contains the first name in the list.

56

- It counts each character in the string, including spaces, punctuation marks, and other special characters and then returns the number of characters in the text string.

Step 2: Press **Enter** to apply the formula. The result should be the length of the name in cell A2 which is 4.

B2			⋮	✕	✓	*fx*	=LEN(A2)	

◢	A	B	C	D	E	F
1	Name	Length				
2	John	4				
3	Jane	4				
4	Imran	5				
5	Kuldeep	7				
6	Michael	7				
7	Christopher	11				
8						

Step 3: Copy the formula down to the other cells in column B. The LEN function has calculated the length of each name in column A and displayed them in column B.

To Summarise

The LEN function is a very useful Excel function and can be used for a wide variety of reasons. For example, if you want to make sure that a password is at least 8 characters long, you can use the LEN function to check the length of the password and return an error message if it does not meet the criteria.

CONCAT Function

What is it?

The CONCAT function in Microsoft Excel is a text function that allows you to combine two or more text strings into a single string. The resulting text string is created by joining the strings together in the order that they are listed. The CONCAT function can be used to concatenate text strings, cell references, and other text or numeric values.

Syntax

=CONCAT(text1, [text2], ...)

Arguments

- **text1** (required): The first text string that you want to concatenate. This can be entered as a string of text enclosed in quotation marks (" "), or as a cell reference to a cell that contains the text you want to concatenate.

- **text2** (optional): The second text string that you want to concatenate. You can include up to 253 additional text strings in the function. Each text string should be separated by a comma.

Example:

Let's say we have a table of data that contains first names and last names in separate columns. The goal is to join the first and last names and enter the full name in column C.

	A	B	C
1	First Name	Last Name	
2	Simon	Smith	
3	Michael	Smith	
4	Bob	Johnson	
5	Bobby	Singh	
6			

Here's how we can do this using the CONCAT function:

C2   ▼   ⋮   ✕   ✓   *fx*   =CONCAT(A2," ",B2)

	A	B	C	D	E
1	First Name	Last Name	Full Name		
2	Simon	Smith	Simon Smith		
3	Michael	Smith			
4	Bob	Johnson			
5	Bobby	Singh			
6					

Step 1: In cell C2, enter the formula "**=CONCAT(A2," ",B2)**".

Here is how the formula works:

- Cell A2 is the text1 argument and is the first name we want to concatenate.

- The text2 argument is the double quotation marks (" ") which adds a space between the first and last name.

- Cell B2 is the text3 argument and is the last name we want to concatenate.

Step 2: Press **Enter** on your keyboard to apply the formula to the cell.

C2   ▼   ⋮   ✕   ✓   *fx*   =CONCAT(A2," ",B2)

	A	B	C	D	E
1	First Name	Last Name	Full Name		
2	Simon	Smith	Simon Smith		
3	Michael	Smith	Michael Smith		
4	Bob	Johnson	Bob Johnson		
5	Bobby	Singh	Bobby Singh		
6					
7					

Step 3: Copy the formula down to the other cells in column C. As you can see, the CONCAT function has joined the first and last names together into a single string in the new "Full Name" column.

CONCAT vs CONCATENTATE Functions

There is another Excel function that also joins text together called CONCATENTATE. Both the CONCAT and CONCATENTATE join two or more text strings into a single text string. However, there is a difference in the way these functions are used.

The CONCAT function was introduced in Excel 2016 and is a simplified version of the CONCATENATE function. The main difference between the two is that CONCAT can handle ranges or arrays of cell references as inputs, whereas CONCATENATE can only accept up to 30 individual cell references or text strings as arguments.

To illustrate this point, let's say we have a list of first names again in column A and we want to combine these names into one in cell C2.

C2	▼	:	✕ ✓	*fx*	=CONCAT(A2:A5)		
	A	B		C		D	E
1	First Name		First Name				
2	Simon		SimonMichaelBobBobby				
3	Michael						
4	Bob						
5	Bobby						
6							

When we use the CONCAT function, we can use the formula "**=CONCAT(A2:A5)**". This function concatenates the four cell values into a single string.

C2	▼	:	✕ ✓	*fx*	=CONCATENATE(A2&A3&A4&A5)		
	A	B		C		D	E	F
1	First Name		First Name				
2	Simon		SimonMichaelBobBobby				
3	Michael						
4	Bob						
5	Bobby						
6							

On the other hand, if we use CONCATENATE with the same input range, we would need to specify each cell reference individually as follows, "**=CONCATENATE(A2&A3&A4&A5)**".

In other words, CONCAT is a more versatile function that can handle a larger number of input references, while CONCATENATE is more limited in its input capabilities.

TEXTJOIN Function

What is it?

The Excel TEXTJOIN function is used to concatenate text from multiple cells or ranges, with a specified delimiter separating each piece of text. It was introduced in Excel 2019 and Excel 365.

Syntax

=TEXTJOIN(delimiter, ignore_empty, text1, [text2], ...)

Arguments

- **delimiter** (required): The character or characters to use as a separator between each text value. This can be any text value, including spaces, commas, semicolons, etc. This argument cannot be empty, and it is always treated as text.

- **ignore_empty** (required): A logical value (TRUE or FALSE) that specifies whether to ignore or include empty cells in the final text string. If set to TRUE, empty cells are skipped and not included in the result. If set to FALSE, empty cells are included in the result.

- **text1** (required): The first piece of text to concatenate. This can be a cell reference, a range of cells, or a text value enclosed in quotation marks.

- **text2, ...** (optional): Additional pieces of text to concatenate. You can include up to 252 text arguments in total.

Example:

Let's say you have a list of fruits and you want to combine them into a single cell separated by commas. Here is what the data looks like:

	A	B
1	Fruit	
2	Apples	
3	Bananas	
4	Oranges	
5	Grapes	
6		

Follow the below steps to join all the fruits in one cell separated by commas using the TEXTJOIN function:

	A	B	C	D	E	F
			=TEXTJOIN(",",TRUE,A2:A5)			
1	Fruit					
2	Apples		Apples,Bananas,Oranges,Grapes			
3	Bananas					
4	Oranges					
5	Grapes					
6						

Step 1: Select the cell where you want the combined text to appear. In this example, we'll select cell C2. Type the following formula, "**=TEXTJOIN(",",TRUE,A2:A5)**".

Here is how the formula works:

- "," is the delimiter argument that is used to separate the text. In this case, we're using a comma to separate each fruit name.

- The ignore_empty argument is set to TRUE. This tells Excel to ignore any blank cells in the range of cells. This means that if there are any blank cells between the fruit names, they will not be included in the final result.

- The range A2:A5 is the text1 argument. This is the range of cells containing the text you want to join.

Step 2: Press **Enter** on your keyboard to apply the formula to cell C2. The result should be the combined text with commas separating the fruit names.

Note: The TEXTJOIN function is only available in Excel 365 and Excel 2019. If you are using an earlier version of Excel, you can use the CONCATENATE function to achieve a similar result.

To Summarise

The TEXTJOIN function in Excel is a useful tool for combining text strings in a range of cells into a single cell, separated by a specified delimiter. By using the TEXTJOIN function, you can save time and effort in manually joining text strings, especially when dealing with large amounts of data. The function is flexible and can be customised to meet your specific needs, whether you want to include or exclude empty cells, or use a different delimiter.

TRIM Function

What is it?

The Excel TRIM function is used to remove leading and trailing spaces from a given text string. It can also remove other non-printable characters such as line breaks, tabs, and carriage returns.

Syntax

=TRIM(text)

Arguments

- **text** (required): The text string that you want to trim. It can be a cell reference, or a text string enclosed in quotation marks.

Example:

Suppose you have a list of names in an Excel spreadsheet with leading and/or trailing spaces, like this:

	A	B
1	Name	
2	John McDonald	
3	Liz Smith	
4	Becky Cooper	
5	Bhupinder Singh	
6		

You can use the TRIM function to remove those spaces and get a clean list of names. Here's how:

B2			✕ ✓ fx	=TRIM(A2)

	A	B	C
1	Name	Trim Name	
2	John McDonald	John McDonald	
3	Liz Smith		
4	Becky Cooper		
5	Bhupinder Singh		
6			
7			

Step 1: In cell B2, enter the formula "**=TRIM(A2)**".

Here is how the formula works:

- Cell A2 contains the text string that you want to clean up.

- The TRIM function then removes any leading or trailing spaces from the text string. A leading space is a space at the beginning of the text string, and a trailing space is a space at the end of the text string.

- Next, the TRIM function removes any extra spaces between words in the text string. If there are multiple spaces between words, the TRIM function will remove all but one space.

- The cleaned-up text string is then returned by the TRIM function.

Step 2: Press **Enter** to confirm the formula. Excel will now display the cleaned up name for John McDonald in cell B2.

	A	B	C
	B2	▼ : ✕ ✓ *fx*	=TRIM(A2)
1	**Name**	**Trim Name**	
2	John McDonald	John McDonald	
3	Liz Smith	Liz Smith	
4	Becky Cooper	Becky Cooper	
5	Bhupinder Singh	Bhupinder Singh	
6			

Step 3: Copy the formula down to the other cells in column B. As you can see, the TRIM function has removed the leading and/or trailing spaces from each name, making the list cleaner and easier to read.

To Summarise

The trim function is an excellent tool to clean text and therefore make your data easier to work with. Below are a few examples of when you might use the TRIM function in Excel:

- **Cleaning up imported data**: If you're working with data that was imported from another source (e.g. a text file), it's common for the data to include extra spaces, tabs, or other characters that can make it difficult to work with. In this case, you can use the TRIM function to remove those extra characters and make the data cleaner and easier to analyse.

- **Comparing text strings**: When you're comparing text strings in Excel (e.g. to check if two names match), it's important to make sure that the strings are formatted consistently. If one string has extra spaces or other characters that the other string doesn't have, the comparison won't work correctly. By using the TRIM function to remove those extra characters, you can ensure that the strings are formatted consistently and the comparison will be accurate.

- **Formatting text for display**: In some cases, you may want to format text in a certain way for display purposes (e.g. removing extra spaces between words). In this case, you can use the TRIM function to clean up the text and make it look more presentable.

- **Removing unwanted spaces from user input**: If you're building a form or other type of user input interface in Excel, it's common for users to accidentally enter extra spaces before or after their input. By using the TRIM function to remove those extra spaces, you can ensure that the user input is formatted consistently and won't cause errors in your calculations or analysis.

LOWER Function

What is it?

The Excel LOWER function is a text function used to convert letters in a given text string to lowercase. It returns the text in all lowercase letters.

Syntax

=LOWER(text)

Arguments

- **text** (required): This is the text string that you want to convert to lowercase. It can be a reference to a cell or a text string enclosed in double quotation marks.

Example:

Suppose we have a list of products in both uppercase and lowercase letters in column A, and we want to convert them all to lowercase using the LOWER function and display the results in column B.

	A	B
1	Products	
2	LAPTOPS	
3	Television	
4	Mobile Phone	
5	TABLET	
6		

Here are the steps to convert all the text to lowercase:

B2   ✕   ✓   *fx*   =LOWER(A2)

	A	B	C	D	E
1	Products	Lowercase			
2	LAPTOPS	laptops			
3	Television				
4	Mobile Phone				
5	TABLET				
6					
7					

Step 1: In cell B2, enter the formula "**=LOWER(A2)**".

Here is how the formula works:

- Cell A2 is used as the text argument as it is the text string that we want to convert to lowercase.

- The formula will apply the LOWER function to the text in cell A2 and convert it to lowercase, and display the result in cell B2.

Step 2: Press **Enter** to confirm the formula. Excel will convert the text in cell A2 which is all uppercase, to lowercase in cell B2.

	A	B	C	D	E
1	Products	Lowercase			
2	LAPTOPS	laptops			
3	Television	television			
4	Mobile Phone	mobile phone			
5	TABLET	tablet			
6					

Cell B2 contains the formula =LOWER(A2)

Step 3: Copy the formula to the rest of the cells in column B. The LOWER function has changed the text in column A to all lowercase text in column B.

To Summarise

By using this function, users can quickly and easily transform text to lowercase letters. This can be helpful in a variety of scenarios, such as when dealing with data that was entered in all caps. The process of using the LOWER function is simple and straightforward, and it can be applied to a range of cells to quickly convert large amounts of data. It can save time and effort by automating the process of converting text to lowercase, and it can help to ensure that data is consistent and easily readable.

UPPER Function

What is it?

The Excel UPPER function is a text function used to convert letters in a given text string to uppercase. It returns the text in all uppercase letters.

Syntax

=UPPER(text)

Arguments

- **text** (required): This is the text string that you want to convert to uppercase. It can be a reference to a cell or a text string enclosed in double quotation marks.

Example:

Suppose you have a list of names in column A that are all in lowercase, and you want to convert them to uppercase using the UPPER function and display the results in column B.

	A	B
1	Name	
2	bob smith	
3	jane arnold	
4	sarah lee	
5	david taggart	
6		

Here are the steps to covert all the text to uppercase:

	A	B	C	D	E
	B2			=UPPER(A2)	
1	Name	Uppercase			
2	bob smith	BOB SMITH			
3	jane arnold				
4	sarah lee				
5	david taggart				
6					

Step 1: In cell B2, enter the formula "**=UPPER(A2)**".

Here is how the formula works:

- Cell A2 is used as the text argument as it is the text string that we want to convert to uppercase.

- The formula will apply the UPPER function to the text in cell A2 and convert it to uppercase, and display the result in cell B2.

Step 2: Press **Enter** to apply the formula. Excel will convert the text in cell A2 which is all lowercase, to uppercase in cell B2.

	A	B	C	D	E
	B2			=UPPER(A2)	
1	Name	Uppercase			
2	bob smith	BOB SMITH			
3	jane arnold	JANE ARNOLD			
4	sarah lee	SARAH LEE			
5	david taggart	DAVID TAGGART			
6					

Step 3: Copy the formula to the rest of the cells in column B. The UPPER function has changed the text in column A to all uppercase text in column B.

To Summarise

The UPPER function is a useful tool for converting text to a consistent format, especially when working with large amounts of data. If you have a column of text in lower case or mixed case format, you can use the UPPER function to convert all the text to uppercase so that they are consistent and easier to read.

PROPER Function

What is it?

The Excel PROPER function is a text function used to convert the first letter of each word in a given string to uppercase, while converting all other letters to lowercase.

Syntax

=PROPER(text)

Arguments

- **text** (required): The text or reference to a cell containing text that you want to convert. This argument can be up to 255 characters long.

Example:

Suppose you have a list of names in column A that are all in lowercase, and you want to properly capitalise the names so it is in the correct format and display the results in column B. Below is the data:

	A	B
1	Name	
2	bob smith	
3	jane arnold	
4	sarah lee	
5	david taggart	
6		

To do this, use the PROPER function using the steps below:

B2			×	✓	fx	=PROPER(A2)

	A	B	C	D	E
1	Name	Propercase			
2	bob smith	Bob Smith			
3	jane arnold				
4	sarah lee				
5	david taggart				
6					

Step 1: In cell B2, enter the formula "=**PROPER(A2)**".

Here is how the formula works:

- Cell A2 is used as the text argument as it is the text string that we want to convert to proper case.

- The formula will apply the PROPER function to the text in cell A2 and change the first letter of each name in uppercase and leave the rest as lowercase, and display the result in cell B2.

Step 2: Press **Enter** to apply the formula.

B2		▾	:	×	✓	*fx*	=PROPER(A2)	
	A	B		C	D	E	F	
1	Name	Propercase						
2	bob smith	Bob Smith						
3	jane arnold	Jane Arnold						
4	sarah lee	Sarah Lee						
5	david taggart	David Taggart						
6								

Step 3: Copy the formula to the rest of the cells in column B. The PROPER function has changed the text in column A to proper case text in column B.

Note: The PROPER function only converts the first letter of each word to uppercase, so be careful if you have text with acronyms or text that needs to be in all caps.

To Summarise

The Excel PROPER function is a useful tool that can save time and effort when working with text data in a spreadsheet. By capitalising the first letter of each word in a text string, the PROPER function can help standardise the formatting of data and make it easier to read and understand. Whether you are creating titles and headings, or simply cleaning up messy text data, the PROPER function can be a valuable tool in your Excel toolbox. By following the step-by-step instructions provided above, you can easily use the PROPER function to capitalise text in your own spreadsheets and improve the clarity and organisation of your data.

SUBSTITUTE Function

What is it?

The Excel SUBSTITUTE function is a text function used to replace one or all occurrences of a specified text string within a larger text string. It is commonly used to manipulate and clean data in spreadsheets.

Syntax

=SUBSTITUTE(text, old_text, new_text, [instance_num])

Arguments

- **text** (required): This is the text string that contains the characters you want to replace.

- **old_text** (required): This is the text string or character that you want to replace.

- **new_text** (required): This is the new text string or character that you want to replace the old text with.

- **instance_num** (optional): This argument is used to specify which occurrence of the old text you want to replace. If you omit this argument, all occurrences of the old text will be replaced.

Example:

Suppose you have a list of email addresses that you need to clean up. The email addresses have an underscore (_) in the middle of the name, and you want to replace the underscore with a dot (.). Here's the data:

	A	B	C
1			
2		Old Email Address	
3		john_doe@abc.com	
4		jane_smith@abc.com	
5		bob_johnson@abc.com	
6		sarah_white@abc.com	
7		peter_parker@abc.com	
8			

To replace the underscores with a dot, you can use the SUBSTITUTE function by following the steps below:

C3   *fx*   =SUBSTITUTE(B3,"_",".")

	A	B	C	D	E	F
1						
2		Old Email Address	New Email Address			
3		john_doe@abc.com	john.doe@abc.com			
4		jane_smith@abc.com				
5		bob_johnson@abc.com				
6		sarah_white@abc.com				
7		peter_parker@abc.com				
8						

Step 1: In cell C3, enter the formula "**=SUBSTITUTE(B3,"_",".")**".

Here is how the formula works:

- B3 is the cell reference of the text you want to modify.

- "_" is the old text you want to replace. In this case, we want to replace the underscore (_) with a dot (.).

- "." is the new text you want to replace the old text with.

- The SUBSTITUTE function searches the text in cell B3 for the first instance of the old text ("_") and replaces it with the new text ("."). The result is the modified text with the underscore replaced with the dot.

Step 2: Press **Enter** to calculate the formula.

	A	B	C	D	E	F
C3				=SUBSTITUTE(B3,"_",".")		
1						
2		Old Email Address	New Email Address			
3		john_doe@abc.com	john.doe@abc.com			
4		jane_smith@abc.com	jane.smith@abc.com			
5		bob_johnson@abc.com	bob.johnson@abc.com			
6		sarah_white@abc.com	sarah.white@abc.com			
7		peter_parker@abc.com	peter.parker@abc.com			
8						

Step 3: Copy the formula in cell C3 to the rest of the cells in column C. The column now contains the cleaned up email addresses.

To Summarise

The SUBSTITUTE function in Excel is a useful tool for replacing text in a cell with new text. By specifying the cell reference or text to be modified, the old text to be replaced, and the new text to replace the old text with, you can easily modify large sets of data in just a few clicks. In the example provided, we used the SUBSTITUTE function to replace the underscores in a list of email addresses with dots, showing how this function can be used to quickly and efficiently clean up data.

FIND Function

What is it?

The Excel FIND function is used to search for a specific character or substring within a larger string of text, and it returns the position of the first character of the found text. This function is useful when you need to find the location of a specific character or substring within a larger text string.

Syntax

=FIND(find_text, within_text, [start_num])

Arguments

- **find_text** (required): This is the text or character that you want to find within the larger text string.

- **within_text** (required): This is the larger text string that you want to search within.

- **start_num** (optional): This is the starting position within the larger text string where you want to begin the search. If this argument is omitted, the search will begin at the first character of the text string.

Example:

Suppose we have the following data in an Excel spreadsheet:

	A	B
1	Name	
2	Bobby Stevens	
3	Jane McDonald	
4	Jonathon Miller	
5	Ian Smith	
6		

We want to find the position of the space character in each name in column A and display the result in column B. Here are the steps to use the FIND function in this example:

B2   =FIND(" ",A2)

	A	B	C	D
1	Name	Position of Space Character		
2	Bobby Stevens	6		
3	Jane McDonald			
4	Jonathon Miller			
5	Ian Smith			
6				

Step 1: In cell B2, enter the formula "**=FIND(" ",A2)**".

This is how the formula works:

- " " is the first argument, which is the character or text string we want to find. In this case, we want to find the position of the space character, so we enclose a space in double quotes to indicate that we're searching for a space.

- Cell A2 is the second argument, which is the text string we want to search within. In this case, we're searching for the space character in the name in cell A2.

- The FIND function returns the position of the first occurrence of the character or text string within the text string being searched. In this case, it returns the position of the first space character in cell A2.

Step 2: Press **Enter** to calculate the formula. Excel will display the position of the space character in cell A2 (which is 6, since the space is the sixth character in the string Bobby Stevens).

B2   =FIND(" ",A2)

	A	B	C	D	E
1	Name	Position of Space Character			
2	Bobby Stevens	6			
3	Jane McDonald	5			
4	Jonathon Miller	9			
5	Ian Smith	4			
6					

Step 3: Copy the formula in cell B2 to the rest of the cells in the column B. This will apply the formula to each cell in column B, and display the position of the space character in each name.

To Summarise

The Excel FIND function is a powerful tool that allows users to search for a specific character or text string within a larger text string, and return the position of the first occurrence of that character or string. It is a useful function for manipulating and analysing data in Excel, and can be used in a variety of ways to perform tasks such as parsing text, extracting data, and cleaning up data. By following the step-by-step instructions and understanding how the formula works, users can effectively use the FIND function to meet their data analysis needs in Excel.

SEARCH Function

What is it?

The Excel SEARCH function is a text function used to find the position of a specified character or a string of characters within a text string. It returns the position of the first character of the found text.

Syntax

=SEARCH(find_text, within_text, [start_num])

Arguments

- **find_text** (required): This is the substring or the text you want to find within the larger string. It can be a string, number or cell reference.

- **within_text** (required): This is the larger string in which you want to search for the substring. It can also be a string, number or cell reference.

- **start_num** (optional): This specifies the starting position of the search. If omitted, the search starts from the first character of the within_text string. If provided, it specifies the character position in the within_text from which to start the search.

Example:

Suppose we have a list of employee names in a column and we want to find out the position of the substring "son". Here is what the data looks like:

	A	B	C
1	Name	Position of "son"	
2	Jason		
3	Alison		
4	Madison		
5	Carson		
6	Jackson		
7	Harrison		
8	Emma		
9			

We can use the SEARCH function to do this. Here's how:

B2		f_x	=SEARCH("son",A2)			

	A	B	C	D	E	F
1	Name	Position of "son"				
2	Jason	3				
3	Alison					
4	Madison					
5	Carson					
6	Jackson					
7	Harrison					
8	Emma					
9						

Step 1: In cell B2, enter the formula "=**SEARCH("son",A2)**". This formula will search for the substring "son" within the text in cell A2 and return the position of the first character of the substring.

Here is a breakdown of the formula:

- "son" is the text we're searching for (the find_text argument).

- Cell A2 is the text string we're searching within (the within_text argument).

- The formula will locate the first position of when the text "son" starts within the name in cell A2.

Step 2: Press **Enter**. The result will be a number that represents the position of the substring "son" within the text in cell A2, which in this case is 3.

B2		f_x	=SEARCH("son",A2)			

	A	B	C	D	E	F	G
1	Name	Position of "son"					
2	Jason	3					
3	Alison	4					
4	Madison	5					
5	Carson	4					
6	Jackson	5					
7	Harrison	6					
8	Emma	#VALUE!					
9							

Step 3: Copy the formula down to the remaining cells in column B. If the substring is not found, the function will return the #VALUE! error as shown in cell B8 because the text "Emma" does not contain the substring "son".

SEARCH vs FIND Excel Function

Both the FIND and SEARCH functions in Excel are used to find the position of a substring within a text string. However, there is a key difference between the two functions.

The FIND function is case-sensitive, meaning that it will distinguish between uppercase and lowercase letters when searching for the substring. For example, the formula =FIND("B","ABC") will return 2, because "B" appears in the second position of the text string "ABC". But the formula =FIND("b","ABC") will return the #VALUE! error, because "b" does not appear in "ABC".

On the other hand, the SEARCH function is case-insensitive, meaning that it does not distinguish between uppercase and lowercase letters when searching for the substring. For example, the formula =SEARCH("B","ABC") and =SEARCH("b","ABC") will both return 2, because the function ignores case.

REPT Function

What is it?

The Excel REPT function is used to repeat a given text string a certain number of times. It can be used to create repeated characters, symbols, or words to fill a cell or range of cells.

Syntax

=REPT(text, number_of_times)

Arguments

- **text** (required): This specifies the text string to be repeated. It can be a cell reference, a text string, or a formula that returns a text string.

- **number_of_times** (required): This specifies the number of times the text string should be repeated. It can be a numeric value, a cell reference that contains a numeric value, or a formula that returns a numeric value.

Example:

Suppose we have a list of fruit and the numbers sold. Here is what the data looks like:

	A	B	C	D
1	Item	Quantity Sold	Bars	
2	Apples	5		
3	Oranges	3		
4	Bananas	2		
5				

We want to use the REPT function to display a visual representation of the quantity sold of each item in the Bars column, using asterisks (*) as the symbol. Here are the steps to use the REPT function to do this:

Step 1: In cell C2, enter the formula "=**REPT("*",B2)**".

Here is how the formula works:

- The first argument is the text string to be repeated. In this case, it is an asterisk symbol enclosed in double quotation marks: "*".

- The second argument is the number of times the text string should be repeated. In this case, it is the value in cell B2, which contains the quantity of Apples: 5.

- The formula is telling Excel to repeat the asterisk symbol 5 times, which results in a string of 5 asterisks in the Bars column next to the Apples row.

Step 2: Press **Enter** to calculate the formula.

Step 3: Copy the formula to the rest of the cells in column C. Here we can see the number of asterisks for each item based on the number sold.

To Summarise

The REPT function in Excel is a powerful tool that can be used to repeat a text string a specified number of times. By using this function, you can display a visual representation of data in your worksheet using any symbol or text string of your choice. The example provided above shows how to use the REPT function to display the quantity of different fruits sold as a string of asterisks, making it easy to quickly compare the quantity of each item at a glance. Whether you're working with large or small datasets, the REPT function is a useful tool to have in your Excel toolkit.

EXACT Function

What is it?

The Excel EXACT function is a text function that compares two text strings and returns a Boolean value of TRUE or FALSE, depending on whether the strings are exactly the same or not. It is case-sensitive, meaning that uppercase and lowercase letters are treated as different characters.

Syntax

=EXACT(text1, text2)

Arguments

- **text1** (required): The first text string to compare.

- **text2** (required): The second text string to compare.

Example:

Suppose we have a list of fruits in column A and B. Here is what the data looks like:

	A	B	C	D
1	Text 1	Text 2	Match	
2	Apple	apple		
3	Pear	Pear		
4	PEACH	peach		
5	banana	banana		
6				

We want to check if the text in column A matches exactly with the text in column B and then enter the results in column C. To do this we use the Excel EXACT function. Here are the steps to do this:

C2				▾	⋮	✕	✓	*fx*	=EXACT(A2,B2)

	A	B	C	D	E	F	G
1	Text 1	Text 2	Match				
2	Apple	apple	FALSE				
3	Pear	Pear					
4	PEACH	peach					
5	banana	banana					
6							

Step 1: In cell C2, enter the formula "**=EXACT(A2,B2)**".

This is the breakdown of the formula:

- Cell A2 is the text1 argument and the first text we want to compare.

- Cell B2 is the text2 argument and the text we want to compare against text1, i.e. cell A2.

- This formula will compare the text in cells A2 and B2 and return either TRUE or FALSE, depending on whether they match exactly.

Step 2: Press **Enter** to calculate the formula. The result in cell C2 should be FALSE, because the text in cell A2 and B2 are not exactly the same. The EXACT function is case-sensitive, so even though the text is the same, the capitalisation is different.

C2							f_x	=EXACT(A2,B2)	
	A	B	C	D	E	F	G	
1	Text 1	Text 2	Match					
2	Apple	apple	FALSE					
3	Pear	Pear	TRUE					
4	PEACH	peach	FALSE					
5	banana	banana	TRUE					
6								

Step 3: Copy the formula to the rest of the cells in column C to compare the remaining text in column A against the text in column B.

To Summarise

The Excel EXACT function is a powerful tool that allows users to compare two strings of text and determine whether they are exactly the same or not. This function is particularly useful for tasks such as data validation, error checking, and text formatting. By following the step-by-step instructions provided in this example, users can easily incorporate the EXACT function into their Excel spreadsheets to enhance their data analysis capabilities.

Date and Time Functions

Excel provides several built-in functions for working with dates and times. They are useful because they allow you to work with date and time values in a variety of ways, making it easier to analyse and manipulate data. In this chapter, we will explore the most commonly used date and time functions to save you time and effort when performing calculations or analyses.

DATE Function

What is it?

The Excel DATE function is a built-in function that returns the serial number of a date based on the specified year, month, and day. It is commonly used to perform calculations with dates. This number can be formatted as a date using the cell formatting options in Excel.

Syntax

=DATE(year, month, day)

Arguments

- **year** (required): Specifies the year of the date. It can be a number or a reference to a cell that contains a number. The year argument should be in the range of 1900 to 9999.

- **month** (required): Specifies the month of the date. It can be a number or a reference to a cell that contains a number. The month argument should be in the range of 1 to 12.

- **day** (required): Specifies the day of the date. It can be a number or a reference to a cell that contains a number. The day argument should be in the range of 1 to 31, depending on the month and year.

Example:

Let's say that you have a dataset that includes information about different dates and you want to use Excel's DATE function to combine the information into a single date value. For example, let's assume that you have the following information:

	A	B	C	D	E
1	Year	Month	Day	Date	
2	2022	2	15		
3					

To use the DATE function to combine this information into a single date value and enter the result in cell D2, you would follow these steps:

Step 1: In cell D2, enter the formula "**=DATE(A2,B2,C2)**".

Here's a breakdown of how the formula works:

- The first argument of the DATE function is the year. In this example, the year argument is entered as A2, which means that the year value is taken from cell A2 in the worksheet. In this case, the year value is 2022.

- The second argument of the DATE function is the month. In the example, the month argument is entered as B2, which means that the month value is taken from cell B2 in the worksheet. In this case, the month value is 2, which represents February.

- The third argument of the DATE function is the day. In the example, the day argument is entered as C2, which means that the day value is taken from cell C2 in the worksheet. In this case, the day value is 15.

- The DATE function then combines the year, month, and day values to create a new date value.

Step 2: Press **Enter** to calculate the formula. Excel will display the combined date value in the cell that you entered the formula into, which in this case is 15/02/2022.

Step 3: If you want to format the date value you can do so in the **Format Cells** dialog box. To do this select the cell with the date value (in this example, cell D2) and then open the **Format Cells** dialog box by right-clicking the mouse and selecting **Format Cells**. Select the **Number** tab and then **Date** in the left hand side pane and choose the date format you require under **Type**.

To Summarise

The Excel DATE function is a useful tool for combining separate year, month, and day information into a single date value. By following the steps outlined above, you can easily use this function to create a new date value in your Excel worksheets. With the ability to format the date value to suit your needs, the DATE function is a versatile tool that can be used in a wide range of Excel applications. Whether you're using it to track project deadlines, schedule appointments, or analyse data over time, the Excel DATE function is a valuable resource that can help you save time and work more efficiently in your Excel workbooks.

DAY Function

What is it?

The Excel DAY function is a built-in function that is used to extract the day of the month from a given date. It returns an integer value between 1 and 31, depending on the day of the month.

Syntax

=DAY(serial_number)

Arguments

- **serial_number** (required): This argument represents the date whose day you want to extract. It can be entered as a serial number that Excel recognises as a date (e.g., 44219 for 1/1/2021). As a reference to a cell that contains a date or as a formula that returns a valid date.

Example:

Suppose you have a list of dates in column A, and you want to extract the day value from each date and display it in column B.

	A	B	C
1	Date	Day	
2	15/01/2023		
3	20/01/2023		
4	12/02/2023		
5	26/02/2023		
6	02/03/2023		
7	10/03/2023		
8			

To do this we use the Excel DAY function. Here are the steps to do this:

	A	B	C	D	E	F
	B2		fx	=DAY(A2)		
1	Date	Day				
2	15/01/2023	15				
3	20/01/2023					
4	12/02/2023					
5	26/02/2023					
6	02/03/2023					
7	10/03/2023					
8						

Step 1: In cell B2, enter the formula "**=DAY(A2)**".

This is how the formula works:

- The serial_number argument is cell A2.

- This formula will extract the day value from cell A2 and display it in cell B2.

Step 2: Press **Enter** and the formula result will be displayed in cell B2.

	A	B	C	D	E	F
	B2		fx	=DAY(A2)		
1	Date	Day				
2	15/01/2023	15				
3	20/01/2023	20				
4	12/02/2023	12				
5	26/02/2023	26				
6	02/03/2023	2				
7	10/03/2023	10				
8						

Step 3: Now, copy the formula to the rest of the cells in column B. You should now have the day value extracted from each date in column A, displayed in column B.

Below are some points you need to note:

- If the serial_number argument is not a valid date, the DAY function will return the #VALUE! error.

- If the serial_number argument refers to a cell that is empty, the DAY function will return 0.

- If the serial_number argument refers to a date that is before January 1, 1900, the DAY function will return the #VALUE! error.

- If the serial_number argument refers to a date that is after December 31, 9999, the DAY function will return the #VALUE! error.

To Summarise

The Excel DAY function is a useful tool for extracting the day value from a date. By using this function, you can quickly and easily extract the day value from a date and use it in other calculations or analyses. In this example, we demonstrated how to use the Excel DAY function step-by-step to extract the day value from a list of dates and display them in a separate column. With this knowledge, you can now use the Excel DAY function to extract the day value from dates in your own spreadsheets.

DAYS Function

What is it?

The Excel DAYS function is a built-in date and time function used to calculate the number of days between two dates. This function returns the number of days between two dates based on a 365-day year, with 12 months of varying days.

Syntax

=DAYS(end_date, start_date)

Arguments

- **end_date** (required): This is the end date for which you want to calculate the number of days. It must be a valid Excel serial number or a reference to a cell containing a date.

- **start_date** (required): This is the start date from which you want to calculate the number of days. It must be a valid Excel serial number or a reference to a cell containing a date.

Example:

Suppose you want to calculate the number of days between two dates as shown below and enter the result in cell C2.

	A	B	C	D
1	Start Date	End Date	# of Days	
2	01/01/2023	14/03/2023		
3				

Here are the steps to do this using the DAYS function:

C2			×	✓	f_x	=DAYS(B2,A2)

	A	B	C	D	E
1	Start Date	End Date	# of Days		
2	01/01/2023	14/03/2023	72		
3					

Step 1: In cell C2, enter the formula "**=DAYS(B2,A2)**".

Here is how the formula works:

- The function subtracts the start date in cell A2 from the end date in cell B2 to determine the difference between the two dates.

- The result of the subtraction is the number of days between the two dates, which is then returned as the result of the function.

Step 2: Press **Enter** and the result will appear in cell C2. The result should be 72 days, which is the number of days between January 1, 2023, and March 14, 2023.

To Summarise

The DAYS function in Excel is a useful tool for calculating the number of days between two dates. By following the simple steps of entering the start and end dates into cells, and then using the DAYS function, Excel can quickly and easily calculate the number of days in between. This can be especially helpful for tracking durations of projects, calculating interest, or creating schedules.

DAYS360 Function

What is it?

The DAYS360 function in Excel is a date and time function that calculates the number of days between two dates based on a 360-day year, where each month has 30 days. This function is commonly used in financial calculations such as interest accruals and amortisation schedules.

Syntax

=DAYS360(start_date, end_date,[method])

Arguments

- **start_date** (required): This is the starting date of the period for which the days are being calculated.

- **end_date** (required): This is the ending date of the period for which the days are being calculated.

- **method**: (optional) This argument specifies the method used to calculate the days between the two dates. It can be one of the following values:

    o   If omitted or set to 0, the US (NASD) method is used. This method counts the number of days between the start date and the end date, and then adjusts the result to exclude any partial periods that fall outside of the month.

    o   If set to 1, the European method is used. This method counts the number of days between the start date and the end date, and then assumes that each month has 30 days.

    o   If set to 2, the Actual method is used. This method calculates the actual number of days between the start date and the end date, without making any adjustments for partial periods.

Example:

Let's say we have two dates and we want to calculate the number of days between them using the 360-day year method and enter the result in cell C2.

	A	B	C	D
1	Start Date	End Date	# of Days	
2	01/01/2023	14/03/2023		
3				

Here are the steps to do this using the DAYS360 function:

C2				✕ ✓ *fx*	=DAYS360(A2,B2)		

	A	B	C	D	E	F
1	Start Date	End Date	# of Days			
2	01/01/2023	14/03/2023	73			
3						

Step 1: In cell C2, enter the formula "**=DAYS360(A2,B2)**".

Here is how the formula works:

- The start date is 01/01/2023 and the end date is 14/03/2023.

- Since we're using the 360-day year method, each month is assumed to have 30 days. Therefore, January has 30 days, February has 30 days and March has 14 days.

- The DAYS360 function counts the number of days between the start date and the end date, assuming that each month has 30 days.

Step 2: Press **Enter**. The result should appear in cell C2, which is the number of days between the start and end dates using the 360-day year method which is 73.

Note: The DAYS360 function does not take into account leap years and assumes that each year has 360 days, which is not accurate. Therefore, this function is not recommended for general-purpose date calculations.

To Summarise

The Excel DAYS360 function is a useful tool for calculating the number of days between two dates using a 360-day year method, which is commonly used in financial calculations. By assuming that each year has 360 days and each month has 30 days, the function allows you to quickly and easily calculate the number of days between two dates, making it useful for a variety of financial applications. Understanding how the function works can help you to accurately calculate interest accruals, amortisations, and other financial metrics in Excel.

MONTH Function

What is it?

The Excel MONTH function returns the month portion of a date, as an integer value ranging from 1 (January) to 12 (December).

Syntax

=MONTH(serial_number)

Arguments

- **serial_number** (required): This argument represents the date whose month you want to extract. It can be entered as a serial number that Excel recognises as a date (e.g., 44946 for 20/1/2023). As a reference to a cell that contains a date or as a formula that returns a valid date.

Example:

Suppose you have a list of dates in column A, and you want to extract the month value from each date and display it in column B. Here is what the data looks like:

	A	B	C
1	Date	Month	
2	12/01/2022		
3	20/02/2022		
4	28/02/2022		
5	26/03/2023		
6	19/05/2022		
7	10/08/2022		
8	11/09/2022		
9	17/10/2022		
10	10/12/2022		
11			

To do this we use the Excel MONTH function. Here are the steps to do this:

	A	B	C	D	E	F
	B2				=MONTH(A2)	
1	Date	Month				
2	12/01/2022	1				
3	20/02/2022					
4	28/02/2022					
5	26/03/2023					
6	19/05/2022					
7	10/08/2022					
8	11/09/2022					
9	17/10/2022					
10	10/12/2022					
11						

Step 1: In cell B2, enter the formula "**=MONTH(A2)**".

Here is how the formula works:

- Excel first converts the date value in cell A2 into a serial number that represents the number of days since January 1, 1900 (or January 1, 1904, if you're using the Mac version of Excel).

- It then uses this serial number to determine the month of the year and returns the month as a number.

Step 2: Press **Enter** to apply the formula to cell B2. The result should be the number 1, which corresponds to the month of January.

	A	B	C	D	E	F
	B2				=MONTH(A2)	
1	Date	Month				
2	12/01/2022	1				
3	20/02/2022	2				
4	28/02/2022	2				
5	26/03/2023	3				
6	19/05/2022	5				
7	10/08/2022	8				
8	11/09/2022	9				
9	17/10/2022	10				
10	10/12/2022	12				
11						

Step 3: Copy the formula down to the rest of the cells in column B. The resulting data in the column should now display the month number for each date in column A.

Below are some points you need to note regarding the MONTH Excel function:

- If the serial_number argument is not a valid date, the MONTH function will return the #VALUE! error.

- If the serial_number argument refers to a cell that is empty, the MONTH function will return 1.

- If the serial_number argument refers to a date that is before January 1, 1900, the MONTH function will return the #VALUE! error.

- If the serial_number argument refers to a date that is after December 31, 9999, the MONTH function will return the #VALUE! error.

To Summarise

The Excel MONTH function is a powerful tool that allows users to extract the month from a date. By following the simple steps outlined above, users can easily apply this function to their data and quickly obtain the desired results. Whether you are working with financial data, project timelines, or simply need to keep track of important dates, the Excel MONTH function can help you save time and improve your productivity.

YEAR Function

What is it?

The Excel YEAR function is a built-in function that extracts the year from a given date and returns it as a four-digit integer. It is useful when you need to work with the year component of a date separately from the rest of the date.

Syntax

=YEAR(serial_number)

Arguments

- **serial_number** (required): This is the date from which you want to extract the year. It can be entered as a serial number that Excel recognises as a date (e.g., 44946 for 20/1/2023). As a reference to a cell that contains a date or as a formula that returns a valid date.

Example:

Suppose you have a list of dates in column A, and you want to extract the year value from each date and display it in column B. This is what the data looks like:

	A	B	C
1	Date	Year	
2	16/01/2019		
3	14/06/2020		
4	11/08/2020		
5	07/02/2021		
6	19/11/2021		
7	02/09/2022		
8	18/12/2022		
9	06/01/2023		
10	10/02/2023		
11			

To do this we use the Excel YEAR function. Here are the steps to do this:

B2				fx	=YEAR(A2)

	A	B	C	D	E	F
1	Date	Year				
2	16/01/2019	2019				
3	14/06/2020					
4	11/08/2020					
5	07/02/2021					
6	19/11/2021					
7	02/09/2022					
8	18/12/2022					
9	06/01/2023					
10	10/02/2023					
11						

Step 1: In cell B2, enter the formula "**=YEAR(A2)**".

This is how the formula works:

- The YEAR function takes the date value from the serial_number argument, which is cell A2.

- It then extracts the year component, and returns it as a four-digit integer.

Step 2: Press **Enter** to apply the formula to cell B2. The result should be the number 2019, which corresponds to the year of the date in cell A2.

B2				fx	=YEAR(A2)

	A	B	C	D	E	F
1	Date	Year				
2	16/01/2019	2019				
3	14/06/2020	2020				
4	11/08/2020	2020				
5	07/02/2021	2021				
6	19/11/2021	2021				
7	02/09/2022	2022				
8	18/12/2022	2022				
9	06/01/2023	2023				
10	10/02/2023	2023				
11						

Step 3: Copy the formula down to the rest of the cells in column B. The resulting data in the column should now display the year for each date in column A.

Like with the Excel DAY and MONTH functions, the YEAR function also has some limitations:

- If the serial_number argument is not a valid date, the YEAR function will return the #VALUE! error.

- If the serial_number argument refers to a cell that is empty, the YEAR function will return 1900.

- If the serial_number argument refers to a date that is before January 1, 1900, the YEAR function will return the #VALUE! error.

- If the serial_number argument refers to a date that is after December 31, 9999, the YEAR function will return the #VALUE! error.

To Summarise

The Excel YEAR function is a powerful tool that allows you to extract the year component of a given date quickly and easily. By providing a valid date input in the serial_number argument, the function extracts the year component of the date and returns it as a four-digit integer. The YEAR function is particularly useful when you need to work with the year component of a date separately from the rest of the date. Overall, the YEAR function is a valuable function in Excel that can save you time and effort when working with dates and analysing data.

DATEVALUE Function

What is it?

The Excel DATEVALUE function is a built-in function that converts a date in text format to a serial number representing the date in Microsoft Excel. This is useful when you have dates in text format and you need to perform calculations or formatting based on the actual date values.

Syntax

=DATEVALUE(date_text)

Arguments

- **date_text** (required): This is the text string that represents the date you want to convert. It can be entered as a string enclosed in quotation marks (" "), a reference to a cell containing the text string, or a formula that returns a text string. The date_text argument must be in a format that Excel recognises as a valid date, such as "31/12/2022" or "31-Dec-2022".

Example:

Here we have a list of dates in column A which are in text format.

	A	B	C
1	Date	Value	
2	20/10/2021		
3	31/12/2022		
4	15/02/2023		
5			

We need to convert each date represented as text into a serial number that Excel recognises as a date and place it in column B. Here are the steps to do this:

B2   ✕ ✓ f_x =DATEVALUE(A2)

	A	B	C	D	E	F
1	Date	Value				
2	20/10/2021	44489				
3	31/12/2022					
4	15/02/2023					
5						

Step 1: In cell B2, enter the formula "**=DATEVALUE(A2)**".

Here is how the formula works:

- Cell A2 is the date_text argument which we want to convert to a date serial number Excel recognises.

- The formula tells Excel to convert the text in cell A2 to a serial number that represents the date.

Step 2: Press **Enter** to apply the formula to cell B2. Excel will display the serial number for the date in cell B2, which should be 44489.

B2   ✕ ✓ f_x =DATEVALUE(A2)

	A	B	C	D	E	F
1	Date	Value				
2	20/10/2021	44489				
3	31/12/2022	44926				
4	15/02/2023	44972				
5						
6						

Step 3: Copy the formula down to the rest of the cells in the column. The resulting data in column B should now contain the values for each date in column A.

To Summarise

The DATEVALUE function is useful because it allows you to convert dates that are represented as text into a format that Excel can recognise as a date. This can be helpful when you are working with data that has been imported from another source or entered manually as text. Once you have converted the text to a serial number using the DATEVALUE function, you can perform various calculations and analysis on the dates, such as finding the difference between two dates, calculating the number of days between two dates, or determining the day of the week that a date falls on.

In addition, formatting the dates as a recognisable date format makes it easier to read and understand the data, as well as to use functions that rely on date calculations, such as the DAYS, MONTHS, YEAR, DATE functions. Overall, the DATEVALUE function helps you work with dates in Excel more efficiently and accurately by allowing you to convert dates that are represented as text into a format that Excel can understand and use.

DATEDIF Function

What is it?

The Excel DATEDIF function is a date function used to calculate the difference between two dates in years, months, or days. The function is particularly useful when you need to calculate the duration between two events, such as the number of days between a project's start and end dates.

Syntax

=DATEDIF(start_date, end_date, unit)

Arguments

- **start_date** (required): The starting date of the period you want to calculate the difference for. This argument can be entered as a reference to a cell containing a date, or it can be entered as a date entered directly in the formula using double quotes, e.g. "2023-01-01".

- **end_date** (required): The ending date of the period you want to calculate the difference for. This argument follows the same rules as the start_date argument.

- **unit** (required): Specifies the unit of time to use for the calculation. This argument should be entered as a text string enclosed in double quotes, and can be one of the following: "Y" (years), "M" (months), or "D" (days).

Example:

Suppose we have two dates, a start date and an end date for a project. Here is what the data looks like:

	A	B	C
1	Start Date	End Date	
2	01/01/2022	26/02/2023	
3			

We need to identify the difference in days, months and years between the two dates and place the difference in days in column D, the difference in months in column E and the difference in years in column F. Here are the steps to do this:

D2				▼	:	✕	✓	f_x	=DATEDIF(A2,B2,"d")

	A	B	C	D	E	F	G
1	Start Date	End Date		Day	Month	Year	
2	01/01/2022	26/02/2023		421			
3							

Step 1: In cell D2, enter the formula "**=DATEDIF(A2,B2,"d")**" to work out the difference between the two dates in days.

Here is how the formula works:

- Cell A2 is the cell reference to the start date.

- Cell B2 is the cell reference to the end date.

- "d" is the unit argument, indicating that we want to calculate the difference between the two dates in days.

- So, in the example, Excel is taking the two dates in cells A2 and B2 and subtracting the start date from the end date to determine the number of days in between.

Step 2: Press **Enter** to calculate the result in cell D2.

E2				▼	:	✕	✓	f_x	=DATEDIF(A2,B2,"m")

	A	B	C	D	E	F	G
1	Start Date	End Date		Day	Month	Year	
2	01/01/2022	26/02/2023		421	13		
3							

Step 3: In cell E2, enter the formula "**=DATEDIF(A2,B2,"m")**" to work out the difference between the two dates in months. This formula works in the same way as the formula in cell D2. Excel is taking the two dates in cells A2 and B2 and subtracts the start date from the end date to determine the number of months in between.

Step 4: Press **Enter** to calculate the result in cell E2.

	A	B	C		D	E	F	G
1	**Start Date**	**End Date**			**Day**	**Month**	**Year**	
2	01/01/2022	26/02/2023			421	13	1	
3								

F2 — =DATEDIF(A2,B2,"y")

Step 5: In cell F2, enter the formula "**=DATEDIF(A2,B2,"y")**". This time we are just changing the unit argument to a "y" to work out the difference between the two dates in years.

Step 6: Now, press **Enter** to calculate the result in cell F2.

Note: The DATEDIF function is a "hidden" function in Excel, which means that it is not documented in the Excel help files, and is not displayed in the Insert Function dialog box. It's important to note that the DATEDIF function is somewhat quirky and can sometimes return unexpected results. For example, it doesn't handle negative dates or fractional years very well. However, for most simple date calculations, the DATEDIF function is a useful tool in Excel.

To Summarise

Overall, the DATEDIF function in Excel is a useful tool for calculating the difference between two dates in various units of time such as days, months, and years. By using the DATEDIF function, Excel takes the two input dates and subtracts the start date from the end date to determine the difference between them in the specified unit. Although the DATEDIF function has some quirks and limitations, it can be a helpful function for most simple date calculations in Excel.

EDATE Function

What is it?

The Excel EDATE function is a built-in date and time function that allows you to add or subtract a specified number of months from a given date.

Syntax

=EDATE(start_date, months)

Arguments

- **start_date** (required): The starting date from which the function will calculate the result. This argument must be a valid Excel date or a reference to a cell that contains a date.

- **months** (required): The number of months you want to add or subtract from the start_date. This argument must be a positive or negative integer or a reference to a cell that contains a positive or negative integer. A positive value for the months argument will add the specified number of months to the start_date, while a negative value will subtract the specified number of months from the start_date.

Example:

Suppose you have a list of dates in column A, and you want to add 3 months to these dates and display the results in column B. This is what the data looks like:

	A	B	C
1	Date	Add 3 Months	
2	05/06/2022		
3	10/08/2022		
4	02/12/2022		
5	15/02/2023		
6			

Here are the steps to do this:

B2   fx   =EDATE(A2,3)

	A	B	C	D	E	F
1	Date	Add 3 Months				
2	05/06/2022	05/09/2022				
3	10/08/2022					
4	02/12/2022					
5	15/02/2023					
6						

Step 1: In cell B2, enter the formula "**=EDATE(A2,3)**".

Here is a breakdown of the formula:

- The first argument (A2) specifies the start date.

- The second argument (3) specifies the number of months to add to the start date.

Step 2: Press **Enter** to calculate the formula in cell B2. The formula should now display the date that is 3 months after the start date, which in this case is 05/09/2022.

B2   fx   =EDATE(A2,3)

	A	B	C	D	E	F
1	Date	Add 3 Months				
2	05/06/2022	05/09/2022				
3	10/08/2022	10/11/2022				
4	02/12/2022	02/03/2023				
5	15/02/2023	15/05/2023				
6						

Step 3: Copy the formula down to the rest of the cells in column B. The dates should be 3 months after the dates in column A.

To subtract the months from the start date, then simply add a minus before the number in the months argument.

	A	B	C	D	E	F
	Date	Add 3 Months				
2	05/06/2022	05/03/2022				
3	10/08/2022	10/05/2022				
4	02/12/2022	02/09/2022				
5	15/02/2023	15/11/2022				
6						

B2 — =EDATE(A2,-3)

Here, the formula in column B is "**=EDATE(A2,-3)**". As you can see, 3 months have been subtracted from the dates in column A.

To Summarise

As you have seen, the EDATE function is a useful tool for calculating dates that are a specified number of months before or after a given date. With this function, Excel users can save time and effort by automating date calculations and avoiding the need for manual calculations. By following the steps outlined in the examples above, users can easily use the EDATE function to calculate the desired date.

NETWORKDAYS Function

What is it?

The Excel NETWORKDAYS function is a built-in function that calculates the number of working days between two given dates, excluding weekends and holidays. It returns a numerical value that represents the number of working days between the start and end dates.

Syntax

=NETWORKDAYS(start_date, end_date, [holidays])

Arguments

- **start_date** (required): This is the starting date of the time period you want to consider.

- **end_date** (required): This is the end date of the time period you want to consider.

- **holidays** (optional): This is an optional argument that allows you to specify a range of cells that contain a list of holidays that should be excluded from the calculation. Holidays can also be entered as individual dates separated by commas or semicolons.

Example:

Suppose you have a list of start dates in column A and end dates in column B. This is what the data looks like:

	A	B	C	D
1	Start Date	End Date	Working Days	
2	01/01/2023	28/01/2023		
3	03/01/2023	03/02/2023		
4	19/01/2023	12/03/2023		
5				

You want to calculate the number of working days between the start and end dates (excluding weekends) and enter the results in column C. Here are the steps to do this:

C2   *fx*   =NETWORKDAYS(A2,B2)

	A	B	C	D	E	F
1	Start Date	End Date	Working Days			
2	01/01/2023	28/01/2023	20			
3	03/01/2023	03/02/2023				
4	19/01/2023	12/03/2023				
5						

Step 1: In cell C2, enter the formula "**=NETWORKDAYS(A2,B2)**".

Here is a breakdown of the formula:

- Cell A2 is used as the start_date argument.

- Cell B2 is used as the end_date argument.

- The formula takes the start date in cell A2 and the end date in cell B2 and calculates the number of working days between them.

Step 2: Press **Enter** to calculate the result in cell C2. In this example, the result should be 20 (excluding weekends).

C2   *fx*   =NETWORKDAYS(A2,B2)

	A	B	C	D	E	F
1	Start Date	End Date	Working Days			
2	01/01/2023	28/01/2023	20			
3	03/01/2023	03/02/2023	24			
4	19/01/2023	12/03/2023	37			
5						

Step 3: Copy the formula down to the remaining rows of the Working Days column to calculate the number of working days for each row.

Note: Weekends are automatically excluded from the calculation, based on your default settings for the work week. By default, weekends in Excel are considered to be Saturdays and Sundays, but you can customise this setting to include or exclude other days of the week.

To Summarise

The NETWORKDAYS function in Excel is a useful tool for calculating the number of working days between two dates. By using this function, you can easily exclude weekends and holidays to get an accurate count of the number of days that employees have worked or will work. Understanding how to use this function is particularly important for business and financial analysts who need to calculate the number of working days for a variety of purposes such as project timelines, payroll calculations, and performance metrics.

EOMONTH Function

What is it?

The Excel EOMONTH function returns the last day of the month that is a specified number of months before or after a given date. "EOMONTH" stands for "End Of MONTH."

Syntax

=EOMONTH(start_date, months)

Arguments

- **start_date** (required): This is the date for which you want to calculate the end of the month. This argument must be a valid Excel date or a reference to a cell that contains a date.

- **months** (required): This is the number of months before or after the start_date for which you want to calculate the end of the month. This argument must be a whole number. A positive value will return a date in the future, while a negative value will return a date in the past.

Example:

Suppose you have a list of dates in column A, and you want to find the last day of the month for each date in column B. This is the sample data:

	A	B	C
1	Date	End of the Month	
2	01/01/2022		
3	15/02/2022		
4	31/03/2022		
5	10/04/2022		
6	20/05/2022		
7			

Here are the steps to do this:

	A	B	C	D	E	F
1	Date	End of the Month				
2	01/01/2022	31/01/2022				
3	15/02/2022					
4	31/03/2022					
5	10/04/2022					
6	20/05/2022					
7						

B2 — =EOMONTH(A2,0)

Step 1: In cell B2, enter the formula "**=EOMONTH(A2,0)**".

Here is a breakdown of how the formula works:

- Cell A2 is the starting date for which we want to find the last day of the month.

- The second argument, 0, means that we want to find the last day of the same month as the start_date.

- So, the EOMONTH function will return the last day of the month for the date in cell A2.

Step 2: Press **Enter** to calculate the result in cell B2. In this example, the result should be 31/01/2022.

	A	B	C	D	E	F
1	Date	End of the Month				
2	01/01/2022	31/01/2022				
3	15/02/2022	28/02/2022				
4	31/03/2022	31/03/2022				
5	10/04/2022	30/04/2022				
6	20/05/2022	31/05/2022				
7						

B2 — =EOMONTH(A2,0)

Step 3: Copy the formula down to the remaining rows of the column to calculate the last day of the month for each of the dates in column A.

Note: To return the last day of the month in the past from the start date, simply add a minus before the number in the months argument.

To Summarise

The EOMONTH function in Excel is a powerful tool that can help you easily calculate the last day of the month for a given date. By using this function, you can save time and effort that would otherwise be spent manually finding the last day of the month. This function is particularly useful for financial and accounting applications where end-of-month calculations are frequently needed.

TIME Function

What is it?

The Excel TIME function is used to create a time value from individual hour, minute, and second components. It takes in the individual hour, minute, and second components as arguments and returns the corresponding time value.

Syntax

=TIME(hour, minute, second)

Arguments

- **hour** (required): This argument specifies the hour component of the time. The value must be an integer between 0 and 23, or a decimal value that represents a fraction of a 24-hour day.

- **minute** (required): This argument specifies the minute component of the time. The value must be an integer between 0 and 59, or a decimal value that represents a fraction of an hour.

- **second** (required): This argument specifies the second component of the time. The value must be an integer between 0 and 59, or a decimal value that represents a fraction of a minute.

Example:

Here we have values as hours, minutes and seconds in column B.

	A	B	C
1	Hour	10	
2	Minute	30	
3	Second	15	
4			
5	Time:		
6			

We want to create a time value from the individual hour, minute, and second components and display it in cell B5. Here are the steps to do this:

◢	A	B	C	D	E	F	G
1	Hour	10					
2	Minute	30					
3	Second	15					
4							
5	Time:	10:30:15					
6							

Step 1: In cell B5, enter the formula "=**TIME(B1,B2,B3)**".

Here is how the formula works:

- The arguments B1, B2, and B3 are used to specify the hour, minute, and second components of the time value.

- The TIME function then combines these values to create the time value.

Step 2: Press **Enter** to calculate the formula. Cell C5 will display the time value in the default time format.

If you want to change the format of the time value, you can do so by selecting cell B5 and using the **Format Cells** dialog box. For example, you could format the time value as "h:mm:ss AM/PM".

Note: If any of the arguments are provided as decimal values, they will be converted to the appropriate integer value based on the decimal value. For example, a decimal value of 0.5 will be converted to 30 minutes.

To Summarise

The Excel TIME function is a useful tool for creating time values from individual hour, minute, and second components. The function takes in the individual components as arguments and returns the corresponding time value. The TIME function can be especially useful when working with time-based data and calculations in Excel, allowing you to combine separate hour, minute, and second values into a single time value. By understanding the syntax and arguments of the TIME function, you can harness the full power of Excel's time-based functionality in your data analysis and calculations.

TIMEVALUE Function

What is it?

The Excel TIMEVALUE function is a built-in function that converts a time string into a decimal number that represents the fraction of a day. This function is useful for converting text representations of time into a numerical format that can be used in calculations.

Syntax

=TIMEVALUE(time_text)

Arguments

- **time_text** (required): The text string that represents the time you want to convert. The text string must be in a format that Excel can recognise as a time. The format can be either 12-hour time or 24-hour time, and it can include seconds, as well as AM/PM if the time is in 12-hour format.

Example:

Suppose you have a list of time values in your Excel worksheet in column A, but they are currently formatted as text. Here is what the data looks like:

	A	B	C
1	Time	Value	
2	08:00:00		
3	10:00:00		
4	16:00:00		
5	21:00:00		
6			

You want to convert them to a time format in column B so that you can perform calculations on them. You can use the TIMEVALUE function to do this. Below are the steps:

B2 | =TIMEVALUE(A2)

	A	B	C	D	E	F
1	Time	Value				
2	08:00:00	0.333333333				
3	10:00:00					
4	16:00:00					
5	21:00:00					
6						

Step 1: In cell B2 enter the formula "**=TIMEVALUE(A2)**".

Here is how the formula works:

- The function expects the text value to be in a recognisable time format, such as "h:mm AM/PM" or "h:mm:ss AM/PM". If the text value is not in a recognisable time format, the function will return a #VALUE! error.

- When you enter the formula into the cell, Excel evaluates the formula and returns the serial number that corresponds to the time value in the referenced cell. Excel then displays the serial number as a formatted time value, using your chosen time format.

- In this example, Excel will convert the text value to the serial number that represents 08:00 (which is 0.333333333333333) and display it in cell B2.

Step 2: Press **Enter** to apply the formula to the cell.

B2				✓	f_x	=TIMEVALUE(A2)	
	A	B	C	D	E	F	
1	Time	Value					
2	08:00:00	0.333333333					
3	10:00:00	0.416666667					
4	16:00:00	0.666666667					
5	21:00:00	0.875					
6							

Step 3: Copy the formula down to the remaining rows in column B. The time values in column B should now be displayed in the time format.

To Summarise

The Excel TIMEVALUE function is a useful tool for converting text representations of time values into Excel serial numbers that can be used in calculations and other operations. By understanding how the function works and how to use it, you can easily convert your time values to a format that Excel can work with. This can save you time and effort when working with time data in your Excel worksheets.

HOUR Function

What is it?

The Excel HOUR function is a built-in function used to extract the hour from a given time value. It returns a whole number representing the hour portion of the time value, ranging from 0 to 23.

Syntax

=HOUR(serial_number)

Arguments

- **serial_number** (required): This is the time value from which the hour is to be extracted. It can be entered directly as a time value (in the format "hh:mm:ss"), or it can be a reference to a cell containing a time value. The serial_number argument is mandatory, and it must be a valid Excel serial number representing a time between 0:00:00 (12:00:00 AM) and 23:59:59 (11:59:59 PM).

Example:

Let's say you have a column of timestamps in Excel that you'd like to extract the hour from and display it in column B.

	A	B	C
1	Timestamp	Hour	
2	2/28/2023 10:00 AM		
3	2/28/2023 2:30 PM		
4	2/28/2023 6:45 AM		
5	2/28/2023 9:15 PM		
6			

Here's how you could use the HOUR function to do that:

B2 f_x =HOUR(A2)

	A	B	C	D	E	F
1	Timestamp	Hour				
2	28/02/2023 10:00	10				
3	28/02/2023 14:30					
4	28/02/2023 06:45					
5	28/02/2023 21:15					
6						

Step 1: In cell B2 where you want to display the hour, enter the formula "**=HOUR(A2)**".

Here is how the formula works:

- The HOUR function takes the time value in cell A2 as its argument.

- Excel calculates the hour component of the time value in A2.

- The HOUR function returns the hour as an integer value, which is then displayed in the adjacent cell.

Step 2: Press **Enter** to apply the formula to the first cell.

B2 f_x =HOUR(A2)

	A	B	C	D	E
1	Timestamp	Hour			
2	28/02/2023 10:00	10			
3	28/02/2023 14:30	14			
4	28/02/2023 06:45	6			
5	28/02/2023 21:15	21			
6					

To Summarise

The HOUR function in Excel is a useful tool for extracting the hour component from a time value. It takes a single argument, which is the time value from which you want to extract the hour, and returns the hour as an integer value. By using this function, you can easily extract the hour from a column of timestamps and display the results in a separate column. This can be particularly helpful for analysing time-based data, such as monitoring daily or hourly trends.

MINUTE Function

What is it?

The Excel MINUTE function is a built-in function that returns the minute component of a given time value. The minute component represents the minute of the hour as an integer value ranging from 0 to 59.

Syntax

=MINUTE(serial_number)

Arguments

- **serial_number** (required): This argument represents the time value for which you want to extract the minute component. It can be supplied as either a valid Excel serial number, a text string representing a time value, or a reference to a cell containing a time value. If the supplied value is not a valid time value, the MINUTE function will return the #VALUE! error.

Example:

Suppose you have a column with times in Excel that you'd like to extract the minute from and display it in column B. Below is the sample data:

	A	B	C
1	Time	Minute	
2	09:30		
3	10:45		
4	12:55		
5	14:25		
6	17:10		
7			

Here's how you could use the MINUTE function to do that:

	A	B	C	D	E	F
1	Time	Minute				
2	09:30	30				
3	10:45					
4	12:55					
5	14:25					
6	17:10					
7						

B2 — =MINUTE(A2)

Step 1: In cell B2 where you want to display the minute, enter the formula "=**MINUTE(A2)**".

Here is how the formula works:

- The MINUTE function takes the time value in cell A2 as its input and returns the minute value of that time.

- In our example, cell A2 contains the time 9:30 AM. When we apply the MINUTE function to this time value, the function extracts the minute value (which is 30), and returns it as the result.

Step 2: Press **Enter** to apply the formula cell B2.

	A	B	C	D	E	F
1	Time	Minute				
2	09:30	30				
3	10:45	45				
4	12:55	55				
5	14:25	25				
6	17:10	10				
7						

B2 — =MINUTE(A2)

Step 3: Copy the formula down to the remaining rows in column B to extract the minutes from the time values.

To Summarise

The MINUTE function takes a time value as its input and returns the minute value as its output. By applying this function, users can quickly extract minute values from their time data for use in various calculations and analysis. The MINUTE function can be used in conjunction with other Excel functions to perform more complex operations involving time data. Overall, the MINUTE function is a powerful tool for anyone who needs to work with time data in Excel.

SECOND Function

What is it?

The Excel SECOND function is a built-in function that returns the seconds of a given time value. It is useful when you need to extract the seconds portion of a time or when you want to perform calculations based on seconds.

Syntax

=SECOND(serial_number)

Arguments

- **serial_number** (required): This argument can be any valid Excel time format or reference to a cell containing a time value. The function returns the second value of the time provided.

Example:

Let's say we have the following data in an Excel spreadsheet:

	A	B	C	D
1	Date	Time	Second	
2	01/01/2023	10:30:45 AM		
3	01/02/2023	2:15:30 PM		
4	01/03/2023	6:45:20 AM		
5				

We want to extract the seconds from the times in column B and display them in column C. We can do this using the SECOND function. Here's how:

C2			fx	=SECOND(B2)	

	A	B	C	D	E
1	Date	Time	Second		
2	01/01/2023	10:30:45 AM	45		
3	01/02/2023	2:15:30 PM			
4	01/03/2023	6:45:20 AM			
5					

Step 1: In cell C2 where you want to display the second, enter the formula "**=SECOND(B2)**".

Here is how the formula works:

- The function takes only one argument, which is the time value you want to extract the seconds from. In this case, B2 refers to the time value 10:30:45 AM in the Time column.
- The SECOND function extracts the seconds from the time value and returns it as a number. In this case, it returns the value 45 because the time value in B2 is 45 seconds.

Step 2: Press **Enter** to apply the formula in cell C2. The SECOND function will return the number of seconds in the time value in cell B2.

C2			▼	⋮	✕	✓	*fx*	=SECOND(B2)	

◢	A	B	C	D	E
1	Date	Time	Second		
2	01/01/2023	10:30:45 AM	45		
3	01/02/2023	2:15:30 PM	30		
4	01/03/2023	6:45:20 AM	20		
5					

Step 3: Copy the formula from cell C2 to cells C3 and C4. As you can see, the SECOND function has extracted the seconds from the time values in column B and displayed them in column C.

To Summarise

The SECOND function takes only one argument, which is the time value you want to extract the seconds from, and returns the seconds as a number. The function is useful for performing time-based calculations and analysis in Excel. By following the step-by-step instructions provided, users can easily use the SECOND function to extract seconds from time values in their Excel spreadsheets.

WEEKNUM Function

What is it?

The Excel WEEKNUM function returns the week number of a given date. The week number indicates the week of the year in which the date falls. This function is useful in various scenarios, such as project planning, resource allocation, and reporting.

Syntax

=WEEKNUM(serial_number,[return_type])

Arguments

- **serial_number** (required): The date for which you want to get the week number. The date can be entered as a reference to a cell containing a date, a serial number representing a date, or a text string that can be recognised as a date by Excel.

- **return_type** (optional): This argument specifies the type of return value you want. The different return_type options are:

107

- 1 or omitted: The week begins on Sunday and ends on Saturday. The function returns week numbers ranging from 1 to 53.

- 2: The week begins on Monday and ends on Sunday. The function returns week numbers ranging from 1 to 53.

- 11: The week begins on Monday and ends on Sunday. The function returns week numbers ranging from 1 to 54.

- 12: The week begins on Tuesday and ends on Monday. The function returns week numbers ranging from 1 to 54.

- 13: The week begins on Wednesday and ends on Tuesday. The function returns week numbers ranging from 1 to 54.

- 14: The week begins on Thursday and ends on Wednesday. The function returns week numbers ranging from 1 to 54.

- 15: The week begins on Friday and ends on Thursday. The function returns week numbers ranging from 1 to 54.

- 16: The week begins on Saturday and ends on Friday. The function returns week numbers ranging from 1 to 54.

Example:

Suppose you have a list of dates in column A and you want to determine the week number of each date and place it in column B.

	A	B	C
1	Date	Week Number	
2	15/12/2022		
3	31/12/2022		
4	05/01/2023		
5	25/01/2023		
6	06/02/2023		
7	18/02/2023		
8	04/03/2023		
9			

To do this, follow these steps:

B2 f_x =WEEKNUM(A2)

	A	B	C	D	E	F
1	Date	Week Number				
2	15/12/2022	51				
3	31/12/2022					
4	05/01/2023					
5	25/01/2023					
6	06/02/2023					
7	18/02/2023					
8	04/03/2023					
9						

Step 1: In cell B2 enter the formula "**=WEEKNUM(A2)**".

Here is how this formula works:

- A2 is the cell reference to the date for which you want to determine the week number.

- The WEEKNUM function takes this date as its argument and returns the week number of that date based on the ISO week numbering system. The ISO week numbering system is a standard used by many countries around the world.

- The result is a number between 1 and 53, depending on the year and the date provided.

Step 2: Press **Enter**. The week number for the date in cell A2 should now appear in cell B2. In this case, it is 51.

	A	B	C	D	E	F
	Date	Week Number				
2	15/12/2022	51				
3	31/12/2022	53				
4	05/01/2023	1				
5	25/01/2023	4				
6	06/02/2023	6				
7	18/02/2023	7				
8	04/03/2023	9				
9						

B2 — =WEEKNUM(A2)

Step 3: Copy the formula in cell B2 down to the rest of the cells in column B. The week numbers are extracted from the dates in column A.

To Summarise

The Excel WEEKNUM function is a useful tool for determining the week number of a given date based on the ISO week numbering system. By following a few simple steps as shown above, you can easily calculate the week number for each date in your list. This function can be especially useful for tasks such as project management or scheduling, where it may be necessary to track the progress of tasks over a period of weeks. Overall, the WEEKNUM function is a great example of how Excel can help automate tasks and save time for users.

WEEKDAY Function

What is it?

The Excel WEEKDAY function returns a number representing the day of the week (as a serial number) for a given date. By default, the function considers Sunday as the first day of the week and assigns it a value of 1, Monday is 2, and so on.

Syntax

=WEEKDAY(serial_number,[return_type])

Arguments

- **serial_number** (required): This is the date for which you want to find the day of the week. It can be entered as a reference to a cell that contains a date or as a direct input of a date value in the form of a serial number or a text string in a recognised Excel date format.

- **return_type** (optional): This argument specifies the type of result you want to return from the function. It is an optional argument and if not provided, the function will default to returning 1 for Sunday, 2 for Monday, and so on. There are three options for return_type:

  - 1 or omitted: This is the default option that returns numbers from 1 to 7, where Sunday is 1 and Saturday is 7.

  - 2: This option returns numbers from 1 to 7, where Monday is 1 and Sunday is 7.

  - 3: This option returns numbers from 0 to 6, where Sunday is 0 and Saturday is 6.

Example:

Suppose we have a list of dates in column A, and we want to determine which day of the week each date falls on, using the WEEKDAY function.

	A	B	C
1	Date	Week Day	
2	01/03/2023		
3	02/03/2023		
4	03/03/2023		
5	04/03/2023		
6	05/03/2023		
7	06/03/2023		
8	07/03/2023		
9			

To do this, follow these steps to enter the day of the week in column B:

B2   fx   =WEEKDAY(A2)

	A	B	C	D	E	F
1	Date	Week Day				
2	01/03/2023	4				
3	02/03/2023					
4	03/03/2023					
5	04/03/2023					
6	05/03/2023					
7	06/03/2023					
8	07/03/2023					
9						

Step 1: In cell B2 enter the formula "**=WEEKDAY(A2)**".

Here is how this formula works:

- This formula takes the date value in cell A2 and returns the corresponding day of the week as a number (1-7) based on the default return_type value of 1 (Sunday).

- The date in cell A2 falls on a Wednesday which is weekday 4 so therefore the formula returns 4.

Step 2: Press **Enter** to calculate the result.

B2			×	✓	f_x	=WEEKNUM(A2)	
	A	B	C	D	E	F	
1	Date	Week Number					
2	15/12/2022	51					
3	31/12/2022	53					
4	05/01/2023	1					
5	25/01/2023	4					
6	06/02/2023	6					
7	18/02/2023	7					
8	04/03/2023	9					
9							

Step 3: Copy the formula in cell B2 down to the rest of the cells in column B. The week days are extracted from the dates in column A.

To Summarise

The WEEKDAY function in Excel is a useful tool for calculating the day of the week for a given date. It returns a numerical value between 1 and 7, representing the day of the week based on the specified return_type argument. By using this function, you can easily analyse data based on the day of the week, such as calculating weekly trends or organising data by day.

NOW Function

What is it?

The Excel NOW function returns the current date and time, as a serial value.

Syntax

=NOW()

Arguments

The NOW function does not require any arguments because it automatically returns the current date and time. The value returned by this function is updated every time the worksheet is calculated.

Example:

Suppose you have a date in cell A2 like this:

⊿	A	B	C
1	Current Date	Current Date and Time	
2	01/03/2023		
3			

You want to enter the current date and time in cell B2. To do this follow these steps:

B2			✕	✓	*fx*	=NOW()

⊿	A	B	C	D
1	Current Date	Current Date and Time		
2	01/03/2023	01/03/2023 20:05		
3				

Step 1: In cell B2 enter the formula "**=NOW()**".

Here is how the formula works:

- The Excel NOW function returns the current date and time based on the system clock of your computer.

- The function returns a serial number that represents the current date and time in Excel's date/time format.

- This serial number is then displayed as a date and time using a format that you specify in the cell.

Step 2: Press **Enter** to apply the formula in cell B2. The cell should now display the current date and time.

Note: The NOW function updates automatically every time the worksheet is recalculated or opened, so the date and time displayed in the cell will always be current.

How to Change the Date and Time Format

To display the date and time in a more readable format, you can apply a date/time format to the cell using the Format Cells dialog box. For example, you might use the format "dd/mm/yyyy h:mm AM/PM" to display the date and time as 1/3/2023 20:05 PM.

To do this you:

1. Select the cell you want to format.

2. Right-click the mouse and select "Format Cells".

3. In the Format Cells dialog box, select the "Custom" category.

4. In the "Type" field, enter "dd/mm/yyyy h:mm AM/PM".

5. Click "OK".

The date and time will be formatted according to the format you specified.

To Summarise

The Excel NOW function is a simple but useful tool for displaying the current date and time in a worksheet. It's a volatile function that updates automatically every time the worksheet is recalculated, and it returns the date and time based on the computer's system clock. By customising the format of the date and time using the Format Cells dialog box, you can display the information in a way that best suits your needs. Keep in mind that the accuracy of the NOW function is dependent on the accuracy of the system clock, so it's important to ensure that your computer's clock is set correctly.

TODAY Function

What is it?

The Excel TODAY function is a built-in date and time function that returns the current date (today's date) in a cell. It is a useful function for tracking dates, calculating intervals, or for automating certain operations that rely on the current date.

Syntax

=TODAY()

Arguments

The TODAY function does not require any arguments, it only takes an empty pair of parentheses because it automatically returns the current day.

Example:

Here we want to enter the current date in cell A2.

	A	B
1	Current Date	
2		
3		

We use the TODAY function to do this using these steps:

A2			✗	✓	*fx*	=TODAY()

	A	B	C	D	E	F
1	Current Date					
2	01/03/2023					
3						

Step 1: In cell A2 enter the formula "**=TODAY()**".

Here is how the formula works:

- When you enter the function in a cell, Excel will automatically calculate and display the current date based on the computer's system clock.

- The date will be updated every time the workbook is opened or the calculation is refreshed.

Step 2: Press **ENTER** to see the result, which will be today's date in the format of dd/mm/yyyy.

Note: As with the NOW function, you can change the formatting of the date using the Format Cells dialog box.

To Summarise

The TODAY function in Excel is a useful tool for quickly and accurately obtaining the current date. By using this function, users can save time and avoid errors that may occur when manually entering the date. Additionally, the TODAY function can be combined with other functions to perform calculations based on the current date. It takes no arguments and is therefore very simple to use.

Maths Functions

Excel is a powerful tool for mathematical calculations and analysis. It includes a range of built-in functions that can help you perform mathematical calculations with ease. In this chapter, we will discuss the most common mathematical functions that are used.

ROUND Function

What is it?

The Excel ROUND function is a mathematical function used to round a given number to a specified number of decimal places. It is useful in financial modelling and data analysis where the accuracy of decimal places is crucial. The function rounds numbers to the nearest even number when the decimal is 5 (also known as bankers' rounding).

Syntax

=ROUND(number, num_digits)

Arguments

- **number** (required): This is the number that you want to round. It can be a reference to a cell containing a numeric value, or a numerical value typed directly into the formula.

- **num_digits** (required): This is the number of digits to which you want to round the number. If num_digits is positive, the number is rounded to the right of the decimal point. If num_digits is negative, the number is rounded to the left of the decimal point.

Example:

Suppose you have a list of numbers in column A that you want to round to two decimal places in column B using the ROUND function.

	A	B	C
1	Number	2 Decimal Places	
2	12.345		
3	45.678		
4	90.123		
5	54.321		
6	67.89		
7			

Here are the step-by-step instructions:

B2				✕	✓	_fx_	=ROUND(A2,2)	
	A	B		C	D	E	F	
1	Number	2 Decimal Places						
2	12.345	12.35						
3	45.678							
4	90.123							
5	54.321							
6	67.89							
7								

Step 1: In cell B2 enter the formula "**=ROUND(A2,2)**".

Here is how this formula works:

- The number we want to round is in cell A2 so we use this cell for the first argument.

- The second argument in the formula, 2, specifies that we want to round the number to two decimal places.

- The ROUND function takes the number in cell A2 and rounds it to the nearest number with two decimal places. If the number in A2 is exactly halfway between two numbers with two decimal places (for example, 1.005), the function rounds to the nearest even number (so 1.005 would be rounded down to 1.00, while 1.015 would be rounded up to 1.02).

Step 2: Press **Enter** to calculate the result. This will round the number in cell A2 to two decimal places and display the result in cell B2.

B2				✕	✓	_fx_	=ROUND(A2,2)	
	A	B		C	D	E	F	
1	Number	2 Decimal Places						
2	12.345	12.35						
3	45.678	45.68						
4	90.123	90.12						
5	54.321	54.32						
6	67.89	67.89						
7								

Step 3: Copy the formula in cell B2 down to the rest of the cells in column B. The numbers all now have two decimal places.

To Summarise

The Excel ROUND function is a powerful tool that allows you to easily round numbers to a specified number of decimal places. By providing the number to be rounded and the number of decimal places as arguments to the ROUND function, you can quickly round a list of numbers to the desired precision. The ROUND function is particularly useful when dealing with financial data, where rounding to a certain number of decimal places is often required. By following the simple steps outlined in the example above, you can easily round numbers in Excel and improve the accuracy of your calculations.

ROUNDUP Function

What is it?

The Excel ROUNDUP function is used to round a given number up to a specified number of digits. It works by rounding a number to a specified number of digits (the precision argument), and then rounding up to the next highest value. If the decimal value of the number is greater than or equal to 0.5, the function rounds up the number to the next integer value. If the decimal value of the number is less than 0.5, the function leaves the number as it is.

Syntax

=ROUNDUP(number, num_digits)

Arguments

- **number** (required): This is the number you want to round up. It can be a cell reference, a named range, or a constant value.

- **num_digits** (required): This argument specifies the number of decimal places to which you want to round up the number. It must be an integer value, which can be positive or negative.

Example:

Suppose you have the following data in cells A2 through A6:

	A	B	C
1	Number	Roundup	
2	8		
3	11		
4	14		
5	16		
6	19		
7			

We want to round each of these numbers up to the nearest integer and display them in column B. Here's how you can do this using the ROUNDUP function:

	A	B	C	D	E	F	G
1	Number	Roundup					
2	2.3	3					
3	4.4						
4	8.2						
5	1.1						
6	6.5						
7							

B2 | =ROUNDUP(A2,0)

Step 1: In cell B2 enter the formula "**=ROUNDUP(A2,0)**".

Here is a breakdown of the formula:

- The number argument takes the number you want to round up, in this case cell A2.

- The num_digits argument tells you the number of digits to which you want to round up. In our case, we want to round up each number to the nearest integer, so we use 0 as the value for num_digits.

Step 2: Press **Enter** to calculate the result. The result should be 3, because 2.3 rounded up to the nearest integer is 3.

	A	B	C	D	E	F	G
1	Number	Roundup					
2	2.3	3					
3	4.4	5					
4	8.2	9					
5	1.1	2					
6	6.5	7					
7							
8							

B2 | =ROUNDUP(A2,0)

Step 3: Copy the formula in cell B2 to the remaining cells in column B. Cells B2 through B6 should now contain the rounded-up values of the numbers in cells A2 through A6.

To Summarise

The ROUNDUP function in Excel is a useful tool for rounding numbers up to a specified number of digits. It works by taking a number and rounding it up to the next integer, based on the specified number of digits. By using this function, you can easily round up numbers in your Excel spreadsheets without having to manually adjust them.

ROUNDDOWN Function

What is it?

The Excel ROUNDDOWN function is used to round down a given number to a specified number of decimal places. It is a mathematical function that is commonly used in financial and accounting applications.

Syntax

=ROUNDDOWN(number, num_digits)

Arguments

- **number** (required): This is the number that you want to round down. It can be a cell reference, a formula, or a constant value.

- **num_digits** (required): This is the number of digits to which you want to round down the number. It can be a positive or negative integer. If you enter a positive integer, the function will round the number down to that many decimal places. If you enter a negative integer, the function will round the number down to the left of the decimal point.

Example:

Suppose we have a list of numbers in column A and we want to round down all the numbers to the nearest integer value and display them in column B.

	A	B	C
1	Number	Rounddown	
2	3.1415		
3	2.7183		
4	1.618		
5	4.6692		
6	0.6931		
7			

Here's how you can use the ROUNDDOWN function to achieve this:

B2   fx   =ROUNDDOWN(A2,0)

	A	B	C	D	E	F	G
1	Number	Rounddown					
2	3.1415	3					
3	2.7183						
4	1.618						
5	4.6692						
6	0.6931						
7							

Step 1: In cell B2 enter the formula "**=ROUNDDOWN(A2,0)**".

Here is how this formula works:

- Cell A2 is the cell reference of the number we want to round down.

- 0 is the number of decimal places we want to round down to.

- The ROUNDDOWN function simply takes the number in the specified cell reference and rounds it down to the nearest integer value. In the example, the formula rounds down the number in cell A2 to the nearest integer which is 3.

Step 2: Press **Enter** to calculate the result.

B2				×	✓	f_x	=ROUNDDOWN(A2,0)	
	A	B	C	D	E	F	G	
1	Number	Rounddown						
2	3.1415	3						
3	2.7183	2						
4	1.618	1						
5	4.6692	4						
6	0.6931	0						
7								

Step 3: Copy the formula in cell B2 to the remaining cells in column B. As you can see, the ROUNDDOWN function has rounded down each number in the column to the nearest integer.

Note: It's worth noting that the ROUNDDOWN function always rounds down to the nearest specified number of digits, regardless of whether the decimal portion of the number is greater than or equal to 0.5. So, for example, if we had a number like 3.9 and we wanted to round down to the nearest integer, the ROUNDDOWN function would return 3, not 4.

To Summarise

The ROUNDDOWN function in Excel is a useful tool for rounding numbers down to a specified number of digits. By specifying the number of decimal places to round down to, you can quickly and easily round down numbers in a given column or cell reference. The function always rounds down to the nearest specified number of digits, regardless of whether the decimal portion of the number is greater than or equal to 0.5. The ROUNDDOWN function is just one of many mathematical functions available in Excel, and can be combined with other functions and formulas to perform complex calculations and data analysis tasks.

SUM Function

What is it?

The Excel SUM function is a built-in mathematical function that is used to add up a range of numbers in a given spreadsheet. It is one of the most commonly used functions in Excel and is useful for calculating totals and subtotals.

Syntax

=SUM(number1,[number2],...)

Arguments

- **number1** (required): This argument represents the first number or range of cells that you want to add up. You can enter a single value or a range of cells separated by commas or semi-colons.

- **number2** (required): This argument represents additional numbers or ranges that you want to add up. You can include up to 255 additional arguments separated by commas or semi-colons.

Example:

Let's say we have the following data in an Excel spreadsheet:

	A	B	C
1	Item	Quantity	
2	Apple	5	
3	Banana	8	
4	Orange	3	
5	Pineapple	2	
6	Total		
7			

We want to find the total quantity of items in our list and enter the total in cell B6. Here's how you can do this using the SUM function:

B6 f_x =SUM(B2:B5)

	A	B	C	D	E	F
1	Item	Quantity				
2	Apple	5				
3	Banana	8				
4	Orange	3				
5	Pineapple	2				
6	Total	18				
7						

Step 1: In cell B6 enter the formula "=**SUM(B2:B5)**".

This is how the formula works:

- The range B2:B5 is used as the number1 argument.

- This tells Excel to add up the values in cells B2 through to B5 and return the result in the cell where you entered the formula.

Step 2: Press **Enter**. The result, 18, will appear in cell B6.

Note: You can also use the SUM function with a range of cells that aren't next to each other. For example, you could use =SUM(B2,B4,B5) to add up the values in cells B2, B4, and B5, but not in cell B3.

To Summarise

The SUM function in Excel is a simple and powerful tool for adding up ranges of numbers in a spreadsheet. Whether you need to add up a few cells or a large range of data, the SUM function can make the process quick and easy. By understanding how the formula works and following the steps outlined in the above example, you should be able to use the SUM function to add up data in your own Excel spreadsheets.

SUMIF Function

What is it?

The Excel SUMIF function is used to sum a range of values that meet a specific criterion or condition. This function is useful when you want to add up only the values that meet a certain criteria in a range of data.

Syntax

=SUMIF(range, criteria, [sum_range])

Arguments

- **range** (required): The range of cells that you want to apply the criteria against.

- **criteria** (required): The condition that you want to test in the range. It can be a number, text, cell reference, or a logical expression such as ">100", "<=500". If you use a cell reference as the criteria, the function tests the value in that cell against the range.

- **sum_range:** (optional) The range of cells that you want to sum. If this argument is omitted, the function will sum the values in the range.

Example:

Suppose you have a table of sales data for a store, and you want to calculate the total sales for a particular product, let's say Apples. We want to enter the sales of Apples in cell E2.

	A	B	C	D	E	F
1	Product	Sales			Sales	
2	Apples	20		Apples		
3	Oranges	15				
4	Bananas	25				
5	Apples	10				
6	Oranges	5				
7	Bananas	30				
8	Apples	15				
9						

Here's how you can use the SUMIF function to do this:

E2			✕ ✓ f_x	=SUMIF(A2:A8,D2,B2:B8)			

	A	B	C	D	E	F	G	H
1	Product	Sales			Sales			
2	Apples	20		Apples	45			
3	Oranges	15						
4	Bananas	25						
5	Apples	10						
6	Oranges	5						
7	Bananas	30						
8	Apples	15						
9								

Step 1: In cell E2 enter the formula "=**SUMIF(A2:A8,D2,B2:B8)**".

Here's a breakdown of the formula:

- A2:A8: This is the range of cells that's in the Product column. It is the range where we want to check the criteria.

- D2: This is the criteria we're using to filter the data. It is the value that we want to sum. The function will look for this value in the range A2:A8.

- B2:B8: This is the range of cells in the Sales column. It is the range of values that we want to sum, but only for the rows that match the criteria.

- So, the SUMIF function checks each cell in the range A2:A8 to see if it contains the value Apples. If a cell matches the criteria, the function adds the corresponding value in the same row in the range B2:B8 to the total. If a cell does not match the criteria, the corresponding value in the range B2:B8 is not added to the total.

Step 2: Press **Enter** to calculate the formula. You should see the result 45 in cell E2, which is the total sales for Apples.

To Summarise

The SUMIF function in Excel is a powerful tool that allows you to calculate the sum of values based on a specified criteria or condition. It is particularly useful when you need to analyse large datasets or filter data based on specific criteria. By following the steps outlined in the example, you can easily use the SUMIF function in your own spreadsheets to perform calculations and analyse data. Understanding how the function works and the syntax involved can help you to make the most of this tool and improve your productivity in Excel.

SUMIFS Function

What is it?

The Excel SUMIFS function is a mathematical function that allows you to sum values that meet multiple criteria. It is useful when you need to add up values based on several conditions that must be met simultaneously.

Syntax

=SUMIFS(sum_range, criteria_range1, criteria1, [criteria_range2, criteria2], ...)

Arguments

- **sum_range** (required): The range of cells that you want to sum.

- **criteria_range1** (required): The first range of cells that you want to use as criteria.

- **criteria1** (required): The first condition that you want to apply to the criteria_range1.

- **criteria_range2, criteria2, criteria_range3, criteria3** (optional): These are optional arguments that allow you to specify additional criteria ranges and criteria. You can specify up to 127 pairs of criteria ranges and criteria.

Example:

Let's say you have a table of sales data for different products in different regions. The table has columns for Product, Region, and Sales, like this:

	A	B	C	D	E	F	G
1	Product	Region	Sales		Product	A	
2	A	East	100		Region	East	
3	B	East	200		Sales		
4	A	West	150				
5	C	East	50				
6	B	West	100				
7	C	West	75				
8	A	East	75				
9							

You want to find the total sales for Product A in the East region and enter the result in cell F3. Here's how you can use the SUMIFS function to do that:

124

	A	B	C	D	E	F	G	H
F3						=SUMIFS(C2:C8,A2:A8,F1,B2:B8,F2)		
1	Product	Region	Sales		Product	A		
2	A	East	100		Region	East		
3	B	East	200		Sales	175		
4	A	West	150					
5	C	East	50					
6	B	West	100					
7	C	West	75					
8	A	East	75					
9								

Step 1: In cell F3 enter the formula "**=SUMIFS(C2:C8,A2:A8,F1,B2:B8,F2)**".

Here is how this formula works:

- C2:C8 is the range of cells containing the sales data.

- A2:A8,F1 is the criteria range and criteria. This tells Excel to only sum the sales for products that match "A" in the Product column.

- B2:B8,F2 is another criteria range and criteria. This tells Excel to only sum the sales for regions that match "East" in the Region column.

- In our example, the formula tells Excel to look for cells in the Sales column (C2:C8) that meet the following criteria:

  o The cells in the Product column (A2:A8) must be "A".

  o The cells in the Region column (B2:B8) must be "East".

- Excel then finds the cells that meet these criteria, and adds their values together to get the result.

Step 2: Press **Enter** to calculate the result. Cells C2 and C8 are added together, as these are the cells that meet the criteria and returns the result 175.

To Summarise

The SUMIFS function in Excel is a powerful tool for quickly summing values in a range that meet multiple criteria. By using the SUMIFS function, you can easily filter and analyse large data sets without having to manually search for and add up individual values. With the step-by-step example provided above, you should now have a good understanding of how to use the SUMIFS function in your own Excel worksheets.

SUMPRODUCT Function

What is it?

The Excel SUMPRODUCT function is a powerful math and statistical function that allows users to multiply corresponding elements in arrays and then sum the results. It is useful for performing calculations on datasets that contain multiple variables and can be used in a variety of applications such as financial analysis, data analysis, and more.

Syntax

=SUMPRODUCT(array1, [array2], [array3], ...)

Arguments

- **array1** (required): This is the first array or range of cells that will be multiplied and summed.

- **array2** (optional): This is an optional second array or range of cells that will be multiplied and summed. Users can specify up to 255 additional arrays using this argument.

- **array3** (optional): This is an optional third array or range of cells that will be multiplied and summed. Users can specify up to 255 additional arrays using this argument.

Example:

Let's assume you have the following data in an Excel spreadsheet and you want to calculate the total revenue:

	A	B	C
1	Quantity	Price	
2	5	$10.00	
3	3	$12.50	
4	2	$8.75	
5	4	$15.00	
6	Total Revenue		
7			

To calculate the total revenue for each product, you can use the SUMPRODUCT function, which multiplies corresponding elements in arrays and returns the sum of those products. We want to return the total sales in cell B6. Here are the steps to do this:

B6   =SUMPRODUCT(A2:A5,B2:B5)

	A	B	C	D	E	F	G	H
1	Quantity	Price						
2	5	$10.00						
3	3	$12.50						
4	2	$8.75						
5	4	$15.00						
6	Total Revenue	$165.00						
7								

Step 1: In cell B6 enter the formula "**=SUMPRODUCT(A2:A5,B2:B5)**".

Here is how the formula works:

- The function takes two arrays as inputs: the Quantity (A2:A5) and the Price (B2:B5).

- It then multiplies the corresponding values in each array, and then adds up the products.

- For example, the first element in the Quantity array is 5, and the first element in the Price array is $10.00. The SUMPRODUCT function multiplies these two values (5 * $10.00 = $50.00), and then does the same for the remaining elements. Finally, it adds up all the products to get the total revenue of $165.00.

Step 2: Press **Enter**, and the total revenue for all products will be displayed in cell B6.

To Summarise

The SUMPRODUCT function is a useful tool in Excel for multiplying corresponding elements in arrays and obtaining their sum. It can be used for various types of calculations, such as calculating total revenue or finding the weighted average of a set of values. By using this function, you can save time and avoid the need for complicated formulas that involve multiple steps. Overall, understanding how to use the SUMPRODUCT function can help you work more efficiently in Excel and get more out of your data.

ABS Function

What is it?

The Excel ABS function is a built-in mathematical function that returns the absolute value of a number, which is the value of a number without its sign. This means that if a number is negative, the ABS function returns the positive value of that number.

Syntax

=ABS(number)

Arguments

- **number** (required): This is the numeric value for which you want to find the absolute value. If the number is positive or zero, the ABS function returns the same number. If the number is negative, the ABS function returns the positive value of that number. If the argument is not a numeric value, the ABS function returns a #VALUE! error.

Example:

Suppose we have a list of numbers in column A and we want to return the absolute value of these numbers and display them in column B.

	A	B	C
1	Number	Absolute Value	
2	-3		
3	5		
4	-7		
5	2		
6	-9		
7			

Here's how you can do this using the ABS function:

B2 | | × | ✓ | *fx* | =ABS(A2)

	A	B	C	D	E	F
1	Number	Absolute Value				
2	-3	3				
3	5					
4	-7					
5	2					
6	-9					
7						

Step 1: In cell B2 enter the formula "**=ABS(A2)**". This formula will calculate the absolute value of the number in cell B2.

Here is how this formula works:

- The ABS function in Excel simply returns the absolute value of a number. This means that it returns the positive value of a number, regardless of whether it was originally negative or positive.

- This formula calculates the absolute value of the number in cell A2.

- So, if the number in cell A2 is negative (as it is in our example), the ABS formula will return the positive version of that number. In other words, it will flip the sign of the number to make it positive.

- On the other hand, if the number in cell A2 was positive, the ABS formula will simply return the same number, since the absolute value of a positive number is itself.

Step 2: Press **Enter** to calculate the result.

B2 | | × | ✓ | *fx* | =ABS(A2)

	A	B	C	D	E	F
1	Number	Absolute Value				
2	-3	3				
3	5	5				
4	-7	7				
5	2	2				
6	-9	9				
7						

Step 3: Copy the formula in cell B2 down to cells B3 to B5. Excel will now calculate the absolute value of each number in column A and display the results in column B.

To Summarise

The ABS function in Excel is a simple yet powerful tool that can be used to calculate the absolute value of a number. This function is particularly useful when dealing with datasets that contain both positive and negative numbers, as it allows you to easily convert negative values to their positive counterparts. By using the ABS function in Excel, you can quickly and easily calculate the absolute value of a range of numbers, saving you time and reducing the likelihood of errors.

EVEN Function

What is it?

The Excel EVEN function is a built-in function that is used to round a given number up to the nearest even integer. The function takes a numeric value as an input and rounds it up to the nearest even integer.

Syntax

=EVEN(number)

Arguments

- **number** (required): This is the value or reference to a cell that you want to round up to the nearest even integer. The value must be a numeric value. The number can be entered directly into the function, or it can be a reference to a cell that contains the number you want to round up.

Example:

Here we have a list of numbers in column A and we want to return the next nearest even number and display them in column B. Here is a sample dataset:

	A	B	C
1	Number	Even Number	
2	13		
3	21		
4	-15		
5	5		
6			

Here's how you can do this using the EVEN function:

	A	B	C	D	E	F
					=EVEN(A2)	
	A	B	C	D	E	F
1	Number	Even Number				
2	13	14				
3	21					
4	-15					
5	5					
6						

Step 1: In cell B2 enter the formula "=**EVEN(A2)**".

Here is how this formula works:

- The EVEN function takes the number that you specify and checks if it's already an even integer. If it is, it simply returns that number.

- If the number is odd, the function rounds it up to the nearest even integer. To do this, it adds 1 to the number and then rounds it down to the nearest integer. This effectively rounds the number up to the next even integer.

Step 2: Press **Enter** to calculate the result. The EVEN function checks if 13 in cell A2 is already even (which it isn't) and then adds 1 to get 14.

	A	B	C	D	E	F
B2					=EVEN(A2)	
	A	B	C	D	E	F
1	Number	Even Number				
2	13	14				
3	21	22				
4	-15	-16				
5	5	6				
6						

Step 3: Copy the formula in cell B2 down to B5.

To Summarise

The Excel EVEN function is a useful tool for rounding a number up to the nearest even integer. It works by checking if the number is already even and returning it if it is. If the number is odd, the function adds 1 to the number and then rounds it down to the nearest integer to get the next even number. This function is particularly helpful when working with sets of data where even numbers are preferred or required.

MOD Function

What is it?

The Excel MOD function is a mathematical function that calculates the remainder when one number is divided by another number. The MOD function is useful in a variety of situations where you need to perform calculations involving remainders. For example, you can use it to determine whether a number is even or odd, or to calculate the number of working days between two dates. It can also be used in financial calculations, such as calculating the interest on a loan or the yield on a bond.

Syntax

=MOD(number, divisor)

Arguments

- **number** (required): This is the numeric value that you want to divide. It can be a number, cell reference, or formula that evaluates to a number. The number can be positive, negative, or zero.

- **divisor** (required): This is the numeric value that you want to divide the number by. It can be a number, cell reference, or formula that evaluates to a number. The divisor can be positive, negative, or zero, but it cannot be equal to zero. If the divisor is zero, the function will return a #DIV/0! error.

Example:

Suppose you have a list of numbers from 1 to 10 in column A, and you want to find the remainder when each number is divided by 3 and display the results in column B.

	A	B	C
1	1		
2	2		
3	3		
4	4		
5	5		
6	6		
7	7		
8	8		
9	9		
10	10		
11			

Here's how you can do this using the MOD function:

B1						=MOD(A1,3)	
	A	B	C	D	E	F	G
1	1	1					
2	2						
3	3						
4	4						
5	5						
6	6						
7	7						
8	8						
9	9						
10	10						
11							

Step 1: In cell B1 enter the formula "**=MOD(A1,3)**".

Here is how the formula works:

- Cell A1 is the number we want to divide.

- 3 is the divisor. This is the number we want to divide cell A1 by.

- The MOD function takes the value in cell A1 (which is 1), divides it by 3, and returns the remainder.

Step 2: Press **Enter** to calculate the result.

B1						=MOD(A1,3)	
	A	B	C	D	E	F	G
1	1	1					
2	2	2					
3	3	0					
4	4	1					
5	5	2					
6	6	0					
7	7	1					
8	8	2					
9	9	0					
10	10	1					
11							

Step 3: Copy the formula down to the remaining cells in the column. The results in column B will show the remainder when each number in column A is divided by 3.

To Summarise

The Excel MOD function is a useful tool for finding the remainder when one number is divided by another. By using the MOD function, we can easily perform calculations on large datasets and quickly determine the remainder for each number in a list. This can be especially useful in fields like finance, where calculating interest payments or loan repayments often involves finding the remainder when a number is divided by a given period. Overall, the MOD function is a versatile and powerful tool that can help us perform complex calculations in Excel with ease.

RAND Function

What is it?

The Excel RAND function is a built-in function that generates a random number between 0 and 1. This function is commonly used in simulations, games, and other applications that require randomisation.

Syntax

=RAND()

Arguments

The RAND function has no arguments.

Example:

Suppose you want to create some random numbers between 0 and 1 in the range A1:10. Here is how you can do this using the RAND function:

Step 1: In cell A1 enter the formula "**=RAND()**".

How is how this formula works:

- When you enter this formula, Excel will randomly generate a number between 0 and 1.

- The RAND function will generate a new number between 0 and 1 every time the worksheet is recalculated or opened.

A1				▼ ⋮	✕ ✓ f_x	=RAND()	
	A	B	C	D	E	F	
1	0.108423						
2							
3							
4							
5							
6							
7							
8							
9							
10							

Step 2: Press **Enter**.

A1				▼ ⋮	✕ ✓ f_x	=RAND()	
	A	B	C	D	E	F	G
1	0.738317						
2	0.923273						
3	0.805412						
4	0.696666						
5	0.992427						
6	0.212753						
7	0.354959						
8	0.114088						
9	0.450932						
10	0.44495						
11							

Step 3: Copy the formula down to cell A10. The numbers in column A should be different each time you recalculate the sheet (either by pressing F9 or by changing any cell).

Note: Because the RAND function is based on randomisation, the numbers it generates are unpredictable and will change every time the worksheet is recalculated. If you need to generate a set of random numbers that can be reproduced later, you can copy and paste the values that the RAND function generates as values, rather than as formulas.

To Summarise

The Excel RAND function is a useful tool for generating random numbers in a spreadsheet. By following the steps outlined above, you can easily use this function to generate a set of random numbers in Excel. The RAND function is useful in a variety of applications, including statistical analysis, simulations, and modelling. It should be noted, however, that the RAND function generates new random numbers each time the sheet is recalculated, so if you need to keep the same set of numbers, you can copy and paste them as values.

RANDBETWEEN Function

What is it?

The Excel RANDBETWEEN function is a built-in function that generates a random integer between two specified numbers.

Syntax

=RANDBETWEEN(bottom, top)

Arguments

- **bottom** (required): This is the bottom or minimum value of the range from which a random number is to be generated.

- **top** (required): This is the top or maximum value of the range from which a random number is to be generated.

Example:

Suppose you want to create some random numbers in column C between the numbers under the Value 1 and Value 2 columns.

	A	B	C	D
1	Value 1	Value 2	Random Number	
2	1	10		
3	2	20		
4	3	30		
5	4	40		
6	5	50		
7	6	60		
8	7	70		
9	8	80		
10	9	90		
11	10	100		
12				

Here is how you can do this using the RANDBETWEEN function:

	A	B	C	D	E	F	G
1	Value 1	Value 2	Random Number				
2	1	10	2				
3	2	20					
4	3	30					
5	4	40					
6	5	50					
7	6	60					
8	7	70					
9	8	80					
10	9	90					
11	10	100					
12							

C2 — =RANDBETWEEN(A2,B2)

Step 1: In cell C2 enter the formula "=**RANDBETWEEN(A2,B2)**".

Here is how the formula works:

- When this formula is entered into cell C2, Excel will generate a random integer between the values in cells A2 and B2.

- The value of the cell will change each time the worksheet is calculated, which can be triggered by various events such as entering new data or pressing the F9 key.

Step 2: Press **Enter** to complete the formula.

C2 — =RANDBETWEEN(A2,B2)

	A	B	C	D	E	F	G
1	Value 1	Value 2	Random Number				
2	1	10	4				
3	2	20	9				
4	3	30	8				
5	4	40	32				
6	5	50	19				
7	6	60	18				
8	7	70	7				
9	8	80	55				
10	9	90	21				
11	10	100	66				
12							

Step 3: Copy the formula down to cell C11. Column C should now display a list of random numbers between the corresponding values in the Value 1 and Value 2 columns.

Note: The numbers in the Random Number column will change each time the worksheet is recalculated (e.g. by pressing F9 or changing a cell value). This is because the RANDBETWEEN function is designed to generate new random numbers each time it is called.

To Summarise

The RANDBETWEEN function is a useful tool in Excel for generating random numbers between a specified range. By following the steps outlined above, you can easily use this function to generate random numbers for a variety of purposes, such as creating randomised data sets for statistical analysis or generating lottery numbers.

Statistical Functions

Statistical Excel functions are a set of built-in functions in Microsoft Excel that allow you to perform statistical analysis on your data. These functions enable you to perform various statistical calculations such as average, standard deviation, variance, correlation, regression analysis, etc.

AVERAGE Function

What is it?

The Excel AVERAGE function is a built-in function that calculates the average of a range of numbers.

Syntax

=AVERAGE(number1, [number2], ...)

Arguments

- **number1** (required): The first number or range of numbers that you want to calculate the average of.

- **number2** (optional): Represents a second number or range of numbers that you want to include in the calculation. You can include up to 255 additional numbers or ranges.

Example:

Let's say you have a list of numbers that represent the sales for each month of the year, and you want to find the average monthly sales. Here is an example of what the data might look like:

	A	B	C	D	E
1	Month	Sales			
2	Jan	100		Average Sales	
3	Feb	150			
4	Mar	200			
5	Apr	125			
6	May	175			
7	Jun	250			
8	Jul	300			
9	Aug	175			
10	Sep	200			
11	Oct	225			
12	Nov	275			
13	Dec	350			
14					

You want to work out the average sales for the year and enter the result in cell E2. Here's how you can do this using the AVERAGE function:

	A	B	C	D	E	F	G
1	Month	Sales					
2	Jan	100		Average Sales	210		
3	Feb	150					
4	Mar	200					
5	Apr	125					
6	May	175					
7	Jun	250					
8	Jul	300					
9	Aug	175					
10	Sep	200					
11	Oct	225					
12	Nov	275					
13	Dec	350					
14							

E2 = AVERAGE(B2:B13)

Step 1: In cell E2 enter the formula "**=AVERAGE(B2:B13)**". This formula will calculate the average of the sales data in cells B2 through B13.

Here is how the formula works:

- We want to average the sales data in cells B2 through B13, so we specify the range as B2:B13 in the argument.

- Excel calculates the sum of the numbers in the specified range (B2 through B13) and then divides that sum by the total number of cells in the range (12 in this case, since we have 12 months of data).

- The result is the average monthly sales for the year, which is displayed in the cell where we entered the formula.

Step 2: Press **Enter** to complete the formula. The cell should display the average monthly sales, which in this case is 210. You can also format the cell to display the result in a particular format, such as a currency or with a specific number of decimal places, if desired. You can do this using the Format Cells dialog box.

Note: The AVERAGE function ignores text values, empty cells, and cells that contain logical values or errors. If all the arguments are non-numeric, the AVERAGE function returns the #DIV/0! error.

The AVERAGE function can accept different types of arguments, including:

- Individual numbers: For example, =AVERAGE(2, 4, 6) will return the result of (2 + 4 + 6) / 3, which is 4.

- Cell references: For example, =AVERAGE(A1:A5) will calculate the average of the numbers in cells A1 through A5.

- Named ranges: For example, =AVERAGE(Sales) will calculate the average of the numbers in the range named "Sales".
- Arrays: You can use an array of numbers directly as an argument for the AVERAGE function. For example, =AVERAGE({1, 2, 3, 4, 5}) will calculate the average of the numbers in the array.

To Summarise

The Excel AVERAGE function is a powerful tool that enables users to easily calculate the average value of a range of cells in a worksheet. This function is particularly useful in situations where you need to analyse large amounts of data quickly and accurately. By using the AVERAGE function, you can avoid the tedious and time-consuming process of manually calculating averages, saving time and increasing efficiency. Additionally, the AVERAGE function is versatile and can be used with a wide range of arguments, including cell references, ranges, and even other functions. In summary, the Excel AVERAGE function is a valuable feature that makes data analysis easier and more efficient.

AVERAGEIF Function

What is it?

The AVERAGEIF function in Excel calculates the average of a range of values that meet a specified condition. It allows you to specify a criterion or condition based on which the function will calculate the average of the corresponding values.

Syntax

=AVERAGEIF(range, criteria, [average_range])

Arguments

- **range** (required): This is the range of cells that you want to evaluate based on a given condition. It can contain both numbers and text.

- **criteria** (required): This is the condition that you want to apply to the range. It can be a number, text, cell reference, or an expression that evaluates to a number or text. The criteria can also include logical operators (such as >, <, >=, <=, <>, and =) to make more complex conditions.

- **average_range** (optional): This specifies the range of cells that you want to average. If this argument is omitted, the function will average the values in the range.

Example:

Suppose you have a spreadsheet with the following data:

	A	B	C	D	E	F
1	Name	Score				
2	Alice	90		Alice		
3	Bob	85				
4	Carl	75				
5	Dave	80				
6	Alice	95				
7	Carl	70				
8						

You want to calculate the average score for Alice and display it in cell E2. Here's how you can do this using the AVERAGEIF function:

E2				×	✓	f_x	=AVERAGEIF(A2:A7,"Alice",B2:B7)		

	A	B	C	D	E	F	G	H	I
1	Name	Score							
2	Alice	90		Alice	92.5				
3	Bob	85							
4	Carl	75							
5	Dave	80							
6	Alice	95							
7	Carl	70							
8									

Step 1: In cell E2 enter the formula "**=AVERAGEIF(A2:A7,"Alice",B2:B7)**". This tells Excel to calculate the average of all the scores in column B where the corresponding name in column A is Alice.

Here is how the formula works:

- The AVERAGEIF function checks each cell in the range A2:A7 to see if it contains the value Alice. If it does, the corresponding value in the range B2:B7 is included in the average.

- Once all the eligible values have been identified, the function calculates the average of those values and returns the result.

- In this case, the formula will find the scores of the two students named Alice (90 and 95) and ignore the scores of the other students. It will then calculate the average of those scores (which is (90+95)/2 = 92.5) and return the result.

Step 2: Press **Enter** to calculate the result. The average score for Alice should appear in the selected cell (E2 in this example), which is 92.5.

You can use the AVERAGEIF function to calculate averages for other names as well, simply by changing the criterion in the cell, in this case cell D2.

To Summarise

The AVERAGEIF function in Excel is a powerful tool for calculating averages based on a specific criterion. It allows you to easily filter a range of data based on a particular condition, such as a name or a value, and then calculate the average of only the values that meet that condition. By using the AVERAGEIF function, you can quickly and accurately calculate averages for specific subsets of your data, which can be extremely useful in a variety of applications, such as analysing sales data, monitoring student performance, or evaluating the effectiveness of marketing campaigns. Overall, the AVERAGEIF function is a valuable tool that can help you make sense of your data and draw meaningful insights from it.

AVERAGEIFS Function

What is it?

The Excel AVERAGEIFS function is a statistical function that calculates the average of a range of cells based on multiple criteria or conditions. This function allows you to find the average value of a range of cells that meet specified criteria or conditions.

Syntax

=AVERAGEIFS(average_range, criteria_range1, criteria1, [criteria_range2, criteria2], ...)

Arguments

- **average_range** (required): This is the range of cells that contain the values to be averaged.

- **criteria_range1** (required): This is the range of cells that contain the first set of criteria or conditions to be met.

- **criteria1** (required): This is the first set of criteria or conditions that must be met for a cell in the criteria_range1 to be included in the calculation of the average.

- **criteria_range2** (optional): This is an additional range of cells that contain a second set of criteria or conditions to be met.

- **criteria2** (optional): This is the second set of criteria or conditions that must be met for a cell in the criteria_range2 to be included in the calculation of the average. You can include up to 127 additional sets of criteria ranges and criteria.

Example:

Let's say we have a dataset that contains information about the number of products sold, the revenue generated, and the region where the sales were made. We want to calculate the average revenue generated by a certain region for a certain range of products.

	A	B	C	D	E	F	G
1	Region	Product	Revenue				
2	North	Product A	$100		Region:	North	
3	South	Product B	$200		Product:	Product A	
4	West	Product A	$300		Average Revenue:		
5	East	Product B	$400				
6	North	Product B	$500				
7	South	Product A	$600				
8	West	Product B	$700				
9	East	Product A	$800				
10	North	Product A	$800				
11	South	Product B	$700				
12	West	Product A	$600				
13	East	Product B	$500				
14	North	Product B	$400				
15	South	Product A	$300				
16	West	Product B	$200				
17	East	Product A	$100				
18							

We want to calculate the average revenue generated by the North region for Product A and enter the result in cell F4. Here is how to do this using the AVERAGEIFS function:

F4 f_x =AVERAGEIFS(C2:C17,A2:A17,F2,B2:B17,F3)

	A	B	C	D	E	F	G	H	I
1	Region	Product	Revenue						
2	North	Product A	$100		Region:	North			
3	South	Product B	$200		Product:	Product A			
4	West	Product A	$300		Average Revenue:	$450			
5	East	Product B	$400						
6	North	Product B	$500						
7	South	Product A	$600						
8	West	Product B	$700						
9	East	Product A	$800						
10	North	Product A	$800						
11	South	Product B	$700						
12	West	Product A	$600						
13	East	Product B	$500						
14	North	Product B	$400						
15	South	Product A	$300						
16	West	Product B	$200						
17	East	Product A	$100						
18									

Step 1: In cell F4 enter the formula "**=AVERAGEIFS(C2:C17,A2:A17,F2,B2:B17,F3)**".

Here is how the formula works:

- This formula calculates the average of the Revenue column (C2:C17).

- The Region column (A2:A17) must be North which is referenced in cell F2.

- The Product column (B2:B17) must be Product A which is referenced in cell F3.

- The AVERAGEIFS function then calculates the average of the revenue data in the range C2:C17 that meets all of the specified criteria, which in this case is the average revenue generated by the North region for Product A.

Step 2: Press **Enter** to calculate the result. The average score for the North region for Product A should appear in the selected cell F4, which is $450.

Note: The AVERAGEIFS function can take up to 127 criteria ranges and criteria arguments, making it a very powerful function for analysing data in Excel.

To Summarise

By specifying different criteria ranges and criteria arguments, the AVERAGEIFS function allows you to filter your data to include only the cells that meet specific conditions, and then calculate the average of those filtered cells. This can be very useful for analysing large datasets and gaining insights into your data.

COUNT Function

What is it?

The Excel COUNT function is used to count the number of cells that contain numbers within a given range or array. It does not count blank or text cells.

Syntax

=COUNT(value1,[value2],...)

Arguments

- **value1** (required): Represents the first value or range of values that you want to count. The argument can be entered as a range of cells or as individual values separated by commas.

- **value2** (optional): Represents additional values or ranges of values that you want to count. You can include up to 255 arguments in total.

Example:

Let's say you have a list of students and their grades in a class as shown below:

	A	B	C	D	E
1	Student Name	Grade			
2	John	85		# of students with grades:	
3	Sarah	92			
4	Emily	76			
5	Michael	89			
6	David	91			
7	Rachel				
8	Mark	83			
9	Lisa	77			
10	Adam				
11	Tom	80			
12					

You want to find out how many students received a grade, i.e., how many cells in the Grade column are not blank and then enter the result in cell E2. Here's how you can use the COUNT function to achieve this:

E2			f_x	=COUNT(B2:B11)		

	A	B	C	D	E	F
1	Student Name	Grade				
2	John	85		# of students with grades:	8	
3	Sarah	92				
4	Emily	76				
5	Michael	89				
6	David	91				
7	Rachel					
8	Mark	83				
9	Lisa	77				
10	Adam					
11	Tom	80				
12						

Step 1: In cell E2 enter the formula "**=COUNT(B2:B11)**".

Here's how the formula works:

- The range B2:B11 is the argument for the COUNT function, which tells Excel what cells to count.

- Excel scans the range B2:B11 and counts the number of cells that contain numeric values. In this case, there are 8 cells with numeric values (i.e., grades).

- The COUNT function then returns the result in the selected cell.

Step 2: Press **Enter** to calculate the result. In this case, the result should be 8 since there are 8 cells in the Grade column that are not blank.

Note: If a cell reference or range contains an error value such as #VALUE! or #DIV/0!, it will not be counted.

To Summarise

The COUNT function in Excel is a useful tool for quickly counting the number of cells in a range that contain numeric values. Its simple syntax and straightforward use make it a popular function for data analysis and statistical calculations. The COUNT function is also versatile and can be used in combination with other functions to count cells that meet specific criteria or to perform more complex calculations.

COUNTA Function

What is it?

The Excel COUNTA function is a built-in function that counts the number of cells in a range that are not empty. It can count cells that contain any type of data, including text, numbers, logical values, and errors. If a cell contains a formula that returns an empty string (" "), the COUNTA function will count it as a non-empty cell.

Syntax

=COUNTA(value1, [value2], ...)

Arguments

- **value1** (required): This argument specifies the first value or range of values to count. You can specify a single cell, a range of cells, or an array constant. You can also use a reference to a range of cells or a range name.

- **value2** (optional): These arguments specify additional values or ranges of values to count. You can specify up to 255 arguments.

Example:

Let's say you have a table of employee data, including their names, departments, and job titles.

	A	B	C	D	E	F	G
1	Name	Department	Job Title				
2	John	Marketing	Manager		# of employees:		
3	Sarah	Sales	Sales Associate				
4	Michael	Marketing	Intern				
5	Anna	HR	Recruiter				
6	Jessica	IT	Developer				
7	Kevin	Sales	Manager				
8	Andrew	IT	Manager				
9							

We want to know how many employees there are in total and display the result in cell F2. To do this, you can use the COUNTA function as follows:

	A	B	C	D	E	F
1	Name	Department	Job Title			
2	John	Marketing	Manager		# of employees:	7
3	Sarah	Sales	Sales Associate			
4	Michael	Marketing	Intern			
5	Anna	HR	Recruiter			
6	Jessica	IT	Developer			
7	Kevin	Sales	Manager			
8	Andrew	IT	Manager			
9						

F2 =COUNTA(A2:A8)

Step 1: In cell F2 enter the formula "**=COUNTA(A2:A8)**".

Here's how the formula works:

- The range A2:A8 is the argument for the COUNTA function, which tells Excel what cells to count.

- The COUNTA function then counts the number of non-blank cells in the range A2:A8.

- The COUNTA function returns the result in the selected cell.

Step 2: Press **Enter** to calculate the result. The result should be displayed in cell F2, which in this case is 7.

Note: The COUNTA function differs from the COUNT function, which only counts cells that contain numerical values. The COUNTA function can be useful for counting the number of cells that contain any type of data, including text and logical values.

To Summarise

The COUNTA function in Excel is a useful tool for counting the number of non-blank cells in a given range. By simply selecting the range and entering the COUNTA function with the appropriate range reference, users can quickly determine the number of cells containing data, whether that be text or numbers. This function is particularly useful for tasks such as data analysis, record keeping, and inventory management.

COUNTBLANK Function

What is it?

The Excel COUNTBLANK function is a built-in function that counts the number of blank cells within a given range. This function is useful when you need to know the number of empty cells in a dataset, as it can help you identify gaps in your data or determine if there are any missing values.

Syntax

=COUNTBLANK(range)

Arguments

- **range** (required): The range of cells that you want to count the blank cells from.

Example:

Suppose you have a table of data that looks like this:

	A	B	C	D	E	F
1	Item	Price	Quantity			
2	A	10	2		# of blank prices and quantities :	
3	B		4			
4	C	20				
5	D					
6	E	30	1			
7						

You want to know how many blank cells there are in the Price and Quantity columns and display the result in cell F2. Here's how you can use the COUNTBLANK function to do this:

F2				✕ ✓ fx	=COUNTBLANK(B2:C6)	
	A	B	C	D	E	F
1	Item	Price	Quantity			
2	A	10	2		# of blank prices and quantities :	4
3	B		4			
4	C	20				
5	D					
6	E	30	1			
7						

Step 1: In cell F2 enter the formula "**=COUNTBLANK(B2:C6)**".

Here's how the formula works:

- The range B2:C6 is the argument for the COUNTBLANK function, which tells Excel what cells to count the blank cells.

- The formula then counts the number of cells that are empty in the range B2:C6, and returns the count as the result.

Step 2: Press **Enter** to return the result. In this case, the result is 4 as there are 4 blank cells in the range B2:C6.

Note: The COUNTBLANK function does not count cells that contain formulas that return empty or null values.

To Summarise

The COUNTBLANK function in Excel is a useful tool for counting the number of empty cells within a specified range. By using this function, you can quickly determine if there are any gaps or missing values in your data set.

With its simple syntax and one required argument, the COUNTBLANK function is easy to use and can save you time and effort when working with large sets of data in Excel.

COUNTIF Function

What is it?

The Excel COUNTIF function is a useful tool for counting the number of cells within a range that meet a specified criterion. It is particularly helpful for analysing data and making decisions based on specific conditions.

Syntax

=COUNTIF(range, criteria)

Arguments

- **range** (required): This is the range of cells that you want to count. It can be a single cell or a range of cells.

- **criteria** (required): This is the condition that the cells in the range must meet to be counted. It can be a number, text, cell reference, or a logical expression. You can use operators like "<", ">", "=", "<=", ">=", "<>" to set the criteria.

Example:

Suppose you have a list of names in column A as shown below:

	A	B	C	D	E
1	Name				
2	John		Jane		
3	Jane				
4	Jane				
5	Mark				
6	John				
7	Jane				
8	Lisa				
9					

You want to count the number of times a specific name appears in the list, let's say Jane, and return the result in cell D2. Here is how you can do this using the COUNTIF function:

	A	B	C	D	E	F	G	H
1	Name							
2	John		Jane	3				
3	Jane							
4	Jane							
5	Mark							
6	John							
7	Jane							
8	Lisa							
9								

D2 formula: =COUNTIF(A1:A8,C2)

Step 1: In cell D2 enter the formula "**=COUNTIF(A1:A8,C2)**".

Here's how the formula works:

- The first argument of the COUNTIF function, A1:A8, specifies the range of cells to search. In this case, we want to search the range A1:A8.

- The second argument of the COUNTIF function, cell C2 which contains the text Jane, specifies the criteria to count. In this case, we want to count the number of cells in the range A1:A8 that contain the text Jane.

- So, the COUNTIF function looks at each cell in the range A1:A8, and if the cell contains the text Jane, it adds 1 to the count. Finally, it returns the total count of cells that met the specified criteria.

Step 2: Press **Enter** to calculate the formula. The result should be 3, because the name Jane appears three times in the list.

Note: The criteria argument is case-insensitive, meaning that it will count cells that contain apple, Apple, or APPLE in the same way.

To Summarise

The COUNTIF function in Excel is a simple yet powerful tool for counting cells that meet a specific criterion within a range of cells. It is particularly useful for analysing data and making decisions based on specific conditions. By understanding its syntax and arguments, users can use this function to quickly and easily count the number of cells that meet their criteria.

COUNTIFS Function

What is it?

The Excel COUNTIFS function is a statistical function that counts the number of cells that meet multiple criteria or conditions within a range. This function allows users to count the number of cells that meet a set of criteria and provides more advanced filtering options than the basic COUNT function.

Syntax

=COUNTIFS(range1, criteria1, [range2], [criteria2], ...)

Arguments

- **range1** (required): This is the range of cells to be evaluated for the first condition.

- **criteria1** (required): This is the criteria that the cells in range1 must meet in order to be counted.

- **range2** (optional): This is an additional range of cells to be evaluated for a second condition.

- **criteria2** (optional): This is the criteria that the cells in range2 must meet in order to be counted. You can have up to 127 range/criteria pairs.

Example:

Let's say you have a data set of employees in a company and you want to count the number of employees who work in a certain department and have a certain job title.

	A	B	C	D	E	F	G
1	Employee Name	Department	Job Title				
2	John Smith	Sales	Manager		Department:	Sales	
3	Jane Doe	Marketing	Coordinator		Job Title:	Manager	
4	Mike Johnson	Sales	Representative		Count:		
5	Sarah Lee	HR	Manager				
6	Alex Kim	Sales	Representative				
7	Dave Brown	Marketing	Manager				
8							

We want to count the number of employees who work in Sales with the job title Manager and return the result in cell F4. Here is how to do this using the COUNTIFS function:

F4			f_x	=COUNTIFS(B2:B7,F2,C2:C7,F3)			

	A	B	C	D	E	F	G
1	Employee Name	Department	Job Title				
2	John Smith	Sales	Manager		Department:	Sales	
3	Jane Doe	Marketing	Coordinator		Job Title:	Manager	
4	Mike Johnson	Sales	Representative		Count:	1	
5	Sarah Lee	HR	Manager				
6	Alex Kim	Sales	Representative				
7	Dave Brown	Marketing	Manager				
8							

Step 1: In cell F4 enter the formula "**=COUNTIFS(B2:B7,F2,C2:C7,F3)**".

Here's how the formula works:

- B2:B7 is the range of cells that contains the department names.

- Cell F2 is the criteria that we want to match in the Department column.

- C2:C7 is the range of cells that contain the job titles.

- Cell F3 is the criteria that we want to match in the Job Title column.

- So, this formula counts the number of cells in the range B2:B7 where the cell value is Sales, AND in the range C2:C7 where the cell value is Manager.

Step 2: Press **Enter** to calculate the formula. The result should be 1, as there is only one employee who meets both criteria.

To Summarise

The Excel COUNTIFS function is a powerful tool that allows you to count cells based on multiple criteria. By specifying one or more ranges and their corresponding criteria, COUNTIFS can quickly count the number of cells that meet those criteria. It is a useful function for analysing and summarising large sets of data in Microsoft Excel. By following the steps outlined in the example provided, users can leverage the COUNTIFS function to easily count specific data points in their own Excel spreadsheets.

LARGE Function

What is it?

The Excel LARGE function is a built-in function that is used to return the nth largest value from a given range of values.

Syntax

=LARGE(array, k)

Arguments

- **array** (required): This is a range of values or an array of data that contains the values from which you want to find the nth largest value. The range must contain at least one value, and it can be a range of cells, an array, or a named range.

- **k** (required): This is an integer value that specifies the position of the largest value that you want to return from the array. For example, if you set k to 1, the function will return the largest value in the array. If you set k to 2, it will return the second largest value in the array, and so on.

Example:

Let's say we have the following data in cells A2:A11:

	A	B	C	D	E
1	Data		Rank	Large	
2	5		1		
3	10		2		
4	8		3		
5	6				
6	2				
7	7				
8	9				
9	3				
10	1				
11	4				
12					

We want to find the top three values in this data set using the LARGE function and display them in cells D2 to D4. Here are the steps to do this:

D2   ▾   ⋮   ✕ ✓   *fx*   =LARGE($A$2:$A$11,C2)

	A	B	C	D	E	F	G	H
1	Data		Rank	Large				
2	5		1	10				
3	10		2					
4	8		3					
5	6							
6	2							
7	7							
8	9							
9	3							
10	1							
11	4							
12								

Step 1: In cell D2 enter the formula "**=LARGE($A$2:$A$11,C2)**".

Here's how the formula works:

- A2:A11 s the range of cells or array of values that you want to find the nth largest value from.

- Cell C2 is the position of the value you want to find, in this case it is the largest position.

- So this formula is telling Excel to find the largest value in the range A2:A11.

Step 2: Press **Enter** to calculate the formula. The result should be 10, as it is the largest number in the range A2:A11.

	A	B	C	D	E	F	G	H
1	Data		Rank	Large				
2	5		1	10				
3	10		2	9				
4	8		3	8				
5	6							
6	2							
7	7							
8	9							
9	3							
10	1							
11	4							
12								

D2 cell formula: =LARGE($A$2:$A$11,C2)

Step 3: Copy the formula down to cells D3 and D4. Cell D3 will display the second largest number and cell D4 the third largest number in the range A2:A11.

Note: Notice that the array argument is an absolute cell reference by inserting the dollar signs ($) before the column and row references. This is because we are copying the formula down column D and we want to keep the range in the array argument the same.

To Summarise

The LARGE function in Excel is a powerful tool that can be used to find the nth largest value in a range. It works by sorting the values in the range from largest to smallest and then returning the value at the specified position. By understanding the syntax and usage of the LARGE function, users can efficiently manipulate large data sets and extract relevant information from them.

SMALL Function

What is it?

The Excel SMALL function is a built-in function that returns the nth smallest value in a range or array of numerical data.

Syntax

=SMALL(array, k)

Arguments

- **array** (required): This is the range or array of numerical data from which you want to find the nth smallest value.

- **k** (required): This specifies which nth smallest value you want to find. It can be any positive integer from 1 to the total number of items in the array.

Example:

Let's say we have a dataset of students and their test scores.

	A	B	C	D	E	F
1	Student Name	Test Score		Rank	Test Score	
2	Alice	92		1		
3	Bob	85		2		
4	Charlie	76		3		
5	David	89				
6	Emma	93				
7	Frank	80				
8	Grace	81				
9	Henry	87				
10	Ingrid	94				
11	Jack	78				
12						

We want to find the three smallest test scores using the SMALL function and display them in cells E2 to E4. Here is how to do this using the SMALL function:

E2			✕ ✓ f_x	=SMALL(B2:B11,D2)			
	A	B	C	D	E	F	G
1	Student Name	Test Score		Rank	Test Score		
2	Alice	92		1	76		
3	Bob	85		2			
4	Charlie	76		3			
5	David	89					
6	Emma	93					
7	Frank	80					
8	Grace	81					
9	Henry	87					
10	Ingrid	94					
11	Jack	78					
12							

Step 1: In cell E2 enter the formula "**=SMALL($B$2:$B$11,D2)**".

Here's how the formula works:

- The range B2:B11 is the range of test scores we want to search for the smallest value. This range includes all of the test scores in the dataset.

- The formula will tell Excel to search for the smallest value in the range B2:B11. Since we specified that we wanted the smallest value (using cell D2), Excel returns the smallest value in the range.

Step 2: Press **Enter** to calculate the formula. This will display the first smallest test score, which is 76.

	A	B	C	D	E	F	G
	E2				=SMALL($B$2:$B$11,D2)		
1	Student Name	Test Score		Rank	Test Score		
2	Alice	92		1	76		
3	Bob	85		2	78		
4	Charlie	76		3	80		
5	David	89					
6	Emma	93					
7	Frank	80					
8	Grace	81					
9	Henry	87					
10	Ingrid	94					
11	Jack	78					
12							

Step 3: Copy the formula down to cells E3 and E4. This will fill the next two smallest test scores.

To Summarise

The Excel SMALL function is a powerful tool that can be used to find the nth smallest value in a range of data. It is particularly useful when working with large datasets where it may be difficult to identify the smallest values manually. By specifying the position of the smallest value as the second argument of the function, we can quickly and easily find multiple smallest values within the same range.

MAX Function

What is it?

The MAX function in Microsoft Excel is a built-in function that returns the highest value in a range of cells or a list of numbers.

Syntax

=MAX(number1,[number2],...)

Arguments

- **number1** (required): This is the first number or range of numbers from which to find the maximum value. It can be a cell reference, a named range, an array, or a constant.

- **number2** (optional): This is the second number or range of numbers from which to find the maximum value. You can have up to 255 number arguments.

Example:

Suppose you have a set of numbers in column A, and you want to find the maximum value in that range and display the result in cell D2.

	A	B	C	D
1	Data			
2	5		Max Number	
3	8			
4	12			
5	6			
6	9			
7	4			
8	11			
9				

Here's how you can do it using the MAX function:

D2 — f_x =MAX(A2:A8)

	A	B	C	D	E	F	G
1	Data						
2	5		Max Number	12			
3	8						
4	12						
5	6						
6	9						
7	4						
8	11						
9							

Step 1: In cell D2 enter the formula "=**MAX(A2:A8)**".

Here is how the formula works:

- The MAX function uses the range A2:A8 as the number1 argument.

- The function then evaluates each value in the argument and determines which one is the largest.

- Finally, the function returns the largest value as the result in cell D2.

Step 2: Press **Enter** to see the result. You will see that the maximum value (12) is displayed in cell D2.

Note: If you have more than one range of numbers, you can separate them with commas inside the MAX function. For example, the formula =MAX(A1:A7, C1:C7) would find the maximum value from the ranges A1:A7 and C1:C7.

To Summarise

The MAX function in Excel is a useful tool for finding the maximum value in a range of numbers. By following the steps outlined above, you can easily use the MAX function to find the largest number in a set of values. With its flexibility to handle multiple ranges or arrays of numbers, the MAX function is an essential tool for data analysis and calculations in Excel.

MAXA Function

What is it?

The Excel MAXA function returns the maximum value in a list of numbers or cells, including numbers, text, logical values, and error values. It differs from the MAX function in that it includes text and logical values in its calculation, whereas the MAX function only considers numerical values.

Syntax

=MAXA(number1,[number2],...)

Arguments

- **number1** (required): The first number or range of numbers to evaluate. It can be a reference to a cell, a range of cells, or a constant value.

- **number2** (optional): The second number or range of numbers to evaluate. You can include up to 255 additional numbers or ranges of numbers, separated by commas.

Example:

Suppose you have a set of numbers in an Excel spreadsheet, as shown below:

	A	B	C	D
1	Data			
2	10		Max Number	
3	-5			
4	15			
5	error			
6	8.5			
7				

You want to find the largest value in this set of numbers, including any errors or non-numeric values and display the result in cell D2. Here's how you can use the MAXA function to do this:

	A	B	C	D	E	F	G
1	Data						
2	10		Max Number	15			
3	-5						
4	15						
5	error						
6	8.5						
7							

D2 ⌄ : ✕ ✓ *fx* =MAXA(A2:A6)

Step 1: In cell D2 enter the formula "**=MAXA(A2:A6)**".

Here's how the formula works:

- The formula uses the range A2:A6 as the number1 argument.

- The MAXA function will evaluate each value in the range and compare it to the other values. It considers numeric values to be greater than non-numeric values, with the exception of logical values (TRUE is considered greater than FALSE).

- It then returns the largest value in the range A2:A6, including non-numeric values such as text, logical values (TRUE or FALSE), and error values.

Step 2: Press **Enter** to apply the function and find the maximum value. In this example, the result of the MAXA function would be 15, because that is the largest value in the range A2:A6, even though there is an error value in cell A5.

Note: The MAXA function is similar to the MAX function, which also finds the maximum value in a range of cells. However, the MAX function ignores non-numeric values and returns an error if any value in the range is not a number. The MAXA function is more versatile in that it can handle non-numeric values and still return the maximum value in the range. If there are multiple maximum values in the range, the MAXA function returns the first one it encounters.

To Summarise

The MAXA function in Excel is a useful tool for finding the maximum value in a range of cells, including both numeric and non-numeric values. It allows you to analyse a set of data that may include errors, text, or logical values and still return the maximum value in the range. Compared to the MAX function, which only considers numeric values, the MAXA function is more versatile and can handle a wider range of data types. By understanding how the MAXA function works and how to use it effectively, you can more easily analyse and understand your data in Excel.

MAXIFS Function

What is it?

The Excel MAXIFS function is a statistical function used to find the maximum value from a range of cells that meet certain criteria or conditions. It was introduced in Excel 2019 and is available in Excel for Office 365, Excel for Mac, and Excel Online.

Syntax

=MAXIFS(max_range, criteria_range1, criteria1, [criteria_range2, criteria2], ...)

Arguments

- **max_range** (required): This is the range of cells from which the maximum value is to be found.

- **criteria_range1** (required): This is the first range of cells that contain the criteria or conditions that the data must meet.

- **criteria1** (required): This is the criteria or condition that must be met in the first criteria_range1. It can be a number, text, logical expression, or reference to a cell containing a value.

- **criteria_range2, criteria2** (optional): These are optional additional ranges of cells and criteria that can be used to further narrow down the data to find the maximum value.

Example:

Suppose we have the following table of data:

	A	B	C	D	E	F
1	Name	Age	Score			
2	John	25	85		Max Score:	
3	Jane	30	90			
4	Jack	28	92			
5	Jill	27	88			
6						

We want to find the maximum score for people aged 27 or older and display the result in cell F2. Here's how to do it:

F2   fx   =MAXIFS(C2:C5,B2:B5,">=27")

	A	B	C	D	E	F	G	H
1	Name	Age	Score					
2	John	25	85		Max Score:	92		
3	Jane	30	90					
4	Jack	28	92					
5	Jill	27	88					
6								
7								

Step 1: In cell F2 enter the formula "=**MAXIFS(C2:C5,B2:B5,">=27")**".

Let's break down the formula:

- The first argument (C2:C5) is the range of cells where we want to find the maximum value (in this case, the scores).

- The second argument (B2:B5) is the range of cells where we want to apply the first criterion (in this case, the ages).

- The third argument (">=27") is the criteria we want to apply to the second argument. This means we want to find scores where the corresponding age is greater than or equal to 27.

- So the formula reads: "Find the maximum value in the range C2:C5 where the corresponding value in the range B2:B5 is greater than or equal to 27."

Step 2: Press **Enter** to apply the formula. The maximum score for people aged 27 or older will be displayed in cell F2, which is 92.

Note: The MAXIFS function is similar to the MAX function, but with the added ability to filter by multiple criteria.

To Summarise

The MAXIFS function in Excel is a powerful tool that allows users to find the maximum value in a range based on multiple criteria. By specifying both the range of cells to be analysed and the criteria to be applied, the MAXIFS function can quickly and easily identify the maximum value that meets the specified conditions. By understanding how to use this function, users can save time and increase efficiency in their data analysis tasks.

MIN Function

What is it?

The Excel MIN function is a built-in function that returns the minimum value from a range of cells or a list of numeric values. It can be used to find the lowest score, the smallest price, or any other smallest value in a given range.

Syntax

=MIN(number1,[number2],...)

Arguments

- **number1** (required): Represents the first number or range of numbers from which you want to find the smallest value. You can enter a single value, a cell reference, or a range of cells.

- **number2** (optional): This is the second number or range of numbers from which the minimum value is to be calculated. You can include up to 255 additional numbers or ranges of numbers, separated by commas.

Example:

Let's say we have a list of values that represent the sales figures for a particular company over the last four quarters. We want to find the minimum sales value from this list using the MIN function in Excel and display the result in cell E2.

	A	B	C	D	E
1	Quarter	Sales			
2	Q1	$50,000		Min Sales:	
3	Q2	$45,000			
4	Q3	$48,000			
5	Q4	$42,000			
6					

Here are the steps to do this:

E2				✕ ✓ *fx*	=MIN(B2:B5)		

	A	B	C	D	E	F	G
1	Quarter	Sales					
2	Q1	$50,000		Min Sales:	$42,000		
3	Q2	$45,000					
4	Q3	$48,000					
5	Q4	$42,000					
6							

Step 1: In cell E2 enter the formula "**=MIN(B2:B5)**".

Here is how the formula works:

- The range B2:B5 is used as the number1 argument.

- The formula tells Excel to look at the values in cells B2 through B5, which contain our sales figures for the four quarters.

- The MIN function then evaluates these values and returns the smallest one.

Step 2: Press **Enter** to complete the formula. So in this example, the MIN function has returned the minimum sales value of $42,000, which occurred in Q4.

Note: The MIN function ignores any text or logical values (such as TRUE or FALSE) in the range or list of numbers. If a cell in the range or list contains an error value (such as #N/A or #DIV/0!), the MIN function will return an error value as well.

To Summarise

The Excel MIN function is a built-in function that is used to find the smallest value in a range of cells or an array of values. It takes one required argument, which is the first number or range of numbers from which you want to find the smallest value, and you can include up to 255 additional numbers or ranges of numbers as optional arguments. The MIN function ignores any text or logical values in the range or list of numbers and returns an error value if any of the cells in the range or list contain an error value. This function is helpful when working with numerical data in Excel, as it allows you to quickly determine the smallest value in a set of numbers.

MINIFS Function

What is it?

The Excel MINIFS function is used to find the minimum value in a range of cells that meets one or more specified criteria. It was introduced in Excel 2016 and is available in later versions of Excel.

Syntax

=MINIFS(range, criteria_range1, criteria1, [criteria_range2, criteria2], ...)

Arguments

- **range** (required): Represents the range of cells in which the minimum value is to be found. It can be a range of cells or an array.

- **criteria_range1** (required): Represents the range of cells that contain the first criteria. It can be the same as the range argument or a different range.

- **criteria1** (required): Represents the first criteria that you want to apply to the criteria_range1. It can be a number, text, date, logical expression, cell reference, or another function.

- **criteria_range2, criteria2** (optional): These are optional arguments and can be used to specify additional criteria ranges and criteria. You can add up to 127 pairs of criteria_range and criteria arguments.

Example:

Suppose we have a table of sales data for a company that sells different products in different regions, and we want to find the minimum sales value for a specific product in a specific region.

	A	B	C	D	E	F	G
1	Product	Region	Sales				
2	Widget	East	100		Product:	Gizmo	
3	Widget	West	200		Region:	West	
4	Gizmo	East	150		Min Sales:	50	
5	Gizmo	West	50				
6	Doodad	East	75				
7	Doodad	West	125				
8							

In this example, we want to display the minimum sales in cell F4 for the product Gizmo in the West region. Here are the steps to do this:

| F4 | | | ▼ | ⋮ | × | ✓ | fx | =MINIFS(C2:C7,A2:A7,F2,B2:B7,F3) |

	A	B	C	D	E	F	G	H
1	Product	Region	Sales					
2	Widget	East	100		Product:	Gizmo		
3	Widget	West	200		Region:	West		
4	Gizmo	East	150		Min Sales:	50		
5	Gizmo	West	50					
6	Doodad	East	75					
7	Doodad	West	125					
8								

Step 1: In cell F4 enter the formula "**=MINIFS(C2:C7,A2:A7,F2,B2:B7,F3)**".

Here's a breakdown of the MINIFS function syntax:

- The first argument is the range of cells to evaluate: C2:C7 contains our sales data.

- The second argument is the criteria range for the first condition: A2:A7 contains our product data. We specify Gizmo as the criteria in cell F2.

- The third argument is the criteria range for the second condition: B2:B7 contains our region data. We specify West as the criteria in cell F3.

- The formula evaluates each cell in the range C2:C7 and returns the minimum value that meets both conditions (product = Gizmo and region = West).

- In our example, only one cell (C5) meets both conditions, and its value is 50.

- So essentially, the MINIFS function filters the data based on the criteria provided and returns the minimum value of the filtered data.

Step 2: Press **Enter**. The formula returns 50, which is the minimum sales value for Gizmo in the West region.

To Summarise

The MINIFS function in Excel is a powerful tool for finding the minimum value among cells that meet multiple criteria. It can be used to filter data based on specific conditions and return the minimum value that meets those conditions. This function is particularly useful when working with large datasets and allows for quick and efficient data analysis. By following the step-by-step instructions provided in the example, users can easily utilise the MINIFS function in their own spreadsheets to quickly retrieve the minimum value based on multiple conditions.

MEDIAN Function

What is it?

The Excel MEDIAN function is a statistical function used to calculate the median value in a set of numerical data. The median is the middle value in a range of values, such that half the values are above it and half the values are below it. If there is an odd number of values in the set, the median is the middle value. If there is an even number of values, the median is the average of the two middle values.

Syntax

=MEDIAN(number1,[number2],...)

Arguments

- **number1** (required): The first number or range of numbers for which you want to find the median.

- **number2** (optional): Additional numbers or ranges of numbers that you want to include in the median calculation.

Example:

Let's say we have a dataset of 10 numbers as follows:

	A	B	C	D	E
1	Data				
2	5		Median		
3	7				
4	10				
5	12				
6	3				
7	9				
8	11				
9	15				
10	8				
11	2				
12					

We want to find the median of this dataset using the MEDIAN function in Excel and display the result in cell D2. Here's how to do it:

	A	B	C	D	E	F	G	H
				=MEDIAN(A2:A11)				
1	Data							
2	5		Median	8.5				
3	7							
4	10							
5	12							
6	3							
7	9							
8	11							
9	15							
10	8							
11	2							
12								

Step 1: In cell D2 enter the formula "**=MEDIAN(A2:A11)**".

Here is how the formula works:

- The function takes a range of values as its argument, which can be either a range of cells, in this case A2:A11, or an array of numbers.

- The function then sorts the values in the range from lowest to highest.

- If there are an odd number of values, the median is simply the middle value in the sorted range.

- If there are an even number of values, the median is calculated as the average of the two middle values in the sorted range.

Step 2: Press **Enter** to calculate the median value. The result should be displayed in cell D2 which is 8.5, the median value of the dataset.

To Summarise

the Excel MEDIAN function is a simple yet powerful tool for finding the middle value of a set of data. By following the steps outlined above, you can easily find the median of any list of numbers in an Excel worksheet. Whether you are analysing student grades, sales data, or any other type of numerical information, the MEDIAN function can help you quickly and accurately determine the central value of your data set. By using this function, you can save time and effort in your data analysis tasks, and make more informed decisions based on the insights you gain from your data.

FREQUENCY Function

What is it?

The Excel FREQUENCY function is a statistical function that returns a frequency distribution of values in a set of data. It calculates how often each value occurs within a range of values, and then returns an array that shows the frequency of each value.

Syntax

=FREQUENCY(data_array, bins_array)

Arguments

- **data_array** (required): This is the array or range of input data for which you want to calculate the frequency distribution. The data must be in the form of an array or a reference to a range of cells.

- **bins_array** (required): This is the array or range of intervals or bins that you want to use to create the frequency distribution. The bins must be in the form of an array or a reference to a range of cells.

The function calculates how many values in the data_array fall into each interval or bin specified in the bins_array. It then returns an array of values that represents the frequency distribution.

The size of the returned array is one less than the size of the bins_array. For example, if you have 10 bins, the function will return an array with 9 values, which represents the frequency of values that fall into each bin.

Example:

Suppose we have a dataset of exam scores for a group of students in column A. We want to find out how many students scored within different score ranges as shown in column D and enter the frequency in column E.

	A	B	C	D	E	F
1	Exam Scores		Bins	Score Range	Frequency	
2	85		69	60-69		
3	72		79	70-79		
4	90		89	80-89		
5	68		100	90-100		
6	92					
7	78					
8	80					
9	76					
10	82					
11	88					
12						

We need to enter the bins in order for the FREQUENCY function to work. Column C contains the bins, which is the last number in the score range in column D.

| E2 | | | fx | {=FREQUENCY(A2:A11,C2:C5)} |

	A	B	C	D	E	F	G
1	Exam Scores		Bins	Score Range	Frequency		
2	85		69	60-69	1		
3	72		79	70-79	3		
4	90		89	80-89	4		
5	68		100	90-100	2		
6	92						
7	78						
8	80						
9	76						
10	82						
11	88						
12							

Step 1: Select the range E2:E5 and then enter the formula "**=FREQUENCY(A2:A11,C2:C5)**".

Step 2: Once you type the formula, press **Ctrl+Shift+Enter**. This is because the FREQUENCY function returns an array of values, so you must enter it as an array formula.

Here is how the formula works:

- The data_array is the range of values we want to analyse. In our example, this is the range A2:A11, which contains the scores.

- The bins_array is an array of values that defines the intervals or "bins" we want to count. In our example, this is the range C2:C5.

- The FREQUENCY function returns an array of values that represents how many values in the data_array fall within each bin in the bins_array.

- This means that the FREQUENCY function will count how many scores in the range A2:A11 fall within each of the score ranges in the range D2:D5. The function returns an array of four values, which represent the counts for each score range.

- The result we get in column E is an array of four values that represent how many scores fall within each of the four score ranges. The first value (1) represents the number of scores between 60-69, the second value (3) represents the number of scores between 70-79, the third value (4) represents the number of scores between 80-89, and the fourth value (2) represents the number of scores between 90-100.

To Summarise

The Excel FREQUENCY function is a useful tool for analysing data and counting how many values fall within a range of values or "bins". In this example, we used the FREQUENCY function to count how many scores fell within each of four score ranges. By specifying the score ranges as the bins_array argument and the scores as the data_array argument, the function returned an array of values representing how many scores fell within each range. This allowed us to easily analyse the data and draw conclusions about the distribution of scores. The FREQUENCY function is a powerful tool for data analysis and is commonly used in fields such as statistics, finance, and research.

Information Functions

Information Excel functions help check the type of data or content in a cell and are used to test different characteristics of a cell. In this chapter, we will explore what all the different information functions are, and how to use them in your dataset.

ISBLANK Function

What is it?

The Excel ISBLANK function is used to check whether a cell is empty or not. It returns TRUE if the cell is empty and FALSE if it contains any value or formula.

Syntax

=ISBLANK(value)

Arguments

- **value** (required): This is the cell or range of cells that you want to test for blankness. If the cell or range of cells is blank, the function will return TRUE. If the cell or range of cells contains any value or formula, the function will return FALSE.

Example:

Let's say we have the following data in cells A2 to A7:

	A	B	C
1	Text	ISBLANK?	
2	Hello		
3			
4	World		
5			
6			
7	Excel		
8			

We want to check if each cell is blank or not using the ISBLANK function in column B. Here's how we can do it:

B2				:	×	✓	f_x	=ISBLANK(A2)

	A	B	C	D	E	F	G
1	Text	ISBLANK?					
2	Hello	FALSE					
3							
4	World						
5							
6							
7	Excel						
8							

Step 1: In cell B2 enter the formula "**=ISBLANK(A2)**".

Here is how the formula works:

- Cell A2 is used as the value argument.

- Excel will then evaluate if cell A2 is blank or not and returns either TRUE or FALSE.

Step 2: Press **Enter** to calculate the formula. The result will be displayed as FALSE, since cell A2 is not blank.

B2				:	×	✓	f_x	=ISBLANK(A2)

	A	B	C	D	E	F	G
1	Text	ISBLANK?					
2	Hello	FALSE					
3		TRUE					
4	World	FALSE					
5		TRUE					
6		TRUE					
7	Excel	FALSE					
8							

Step 3: Copy the formula down to cell B7. The results will be displayed as FALSE for cells B2, B4, and B7 (since cells A2, A4 and A7 are not blank), and TRUE for cells B3, B5, and B6 (since cells A3, A5 and A6 are blank).

To Summarise

The Excel ISBLANK function is a useful tool for checking whether a cell is empty or not. By taking a cell or range of cells as input, the function returns a Boolean value (TRUE or FALSE) that indicates whether the cell is empty or not. This can be helpful for a variety of purposes, such as data validation, conditional formatting, and data analysis.

ISERROR Function

What is it?

The Excel ISERROR function is a logical function that checks whether a value is an error value or not. It returns TRUE if the value is an error value (such as #N/A, #VALUE!, #REF!, #DIV/0!, #NUM!, or #NAME?), and FALSE if it is not.

Syntax

=ISERROR(value)

Arguments

- **value** (required): The value that you want to check for an error. This can be a cell reference, a formula, or a value. The function returns TRUE if the value is an error value, and FALSE if it is not.

Example:

Suppose we have a list of numbers in cells A2 to A7, as shown below:

	A	B	C
1	Data	ISERROR?	
2	10		
3	15		
4	#N/A		
5	20		
6	#DIV/0!		
7	25		
8			

We want to check if each value in the list is an error or not using the ISERROR function in column B. Here are the steps:

B2 f_x =ISERROR(A2)

	A	B	C	D	E	F
1	Data	ISERROR?				
2	10	FALSE				
3	15					
4	#N/A					
5	20					
6	#DIV/0!					
7	25					
8						

Step 1: In cell B2 enter the formula "=**ISERROR(A2)**".

Here is how the formula works:

- Cell A2 is used as the value argument.

- Excel evaluates the contents of cell A2 to determine whether it contains an error or not.

- If cell A2 contains an error, such as #N/A or #DIV/0!, the function will return a value of TRUE.

- If cell A2 does not contain an error, the function will return a value of FALSE.

Step 2: Press **Enter** to calculate the formula. The result in cell B2 will be FALSE, since cell A2 does not contain an error.

B2						=ISERROR(A2)	
	A	B	C	D	E	F	
1	Data	ISERROR?					
2	10	FALSE					
3	15	FALSE					
4	#N/A	TRUE					
5	20	FALSE					
6	#DIV/0!	TRUE					
7	25	FALSE					
8							

Step 3: Copy the formula down to cell B7. The results will be displayed as FALSE for cells B2, B3, B5 and B7 (since the corresponding values in column A are not errors), and TRUE for cells B4, and B6 (since the corresponding values in column A are errors).

To Summarise

The ISERROR function is a useful Excel function that helps to determine if a given value is an error or not. It returns a Boolean value of TRUE or FALSE, which can be used to trigger further actions or to simply identify errors in a spreadsheet. By following the steps outlined in the example above, users can effectively use the ISERROR function to check if each value in a list is an error or not. This function can be especially helpful when working with large sets of data or when trying to identify and troubleshoot errors in complex spreadsheets.

ISFORMULA Function

What is it?

The Excel ISFORMULA function is a logical function that checks whether a given cell contains a formula or not. It returns TRUE if the cell contains a formula and FALSE if the cell contains a value or is empty.

Syntax

=ISFORMULA(reference)

Arguments

- **reference** (required): This is the reference to the cell that you want to check if it contains a formula. It can be a cell reference (e.g., A1) or a range of cell references (e.g., A1:C10).

Example:

Let's say we have the following data in cells A2 to A5:

	A	B	C
1	Data	ISFORMULA?	
2	5		
3	=2+2		
4	hello		
5	=SUM(F2:F6)		
6			

We want to check if each value in the list in column A contains a formula or not using the ISFORMULA function in column B. Here are the steps to do this:

B2		× ✓ f_x	=ISFORMULA(A2)			

	A	B	C	D	E	F
1	Data	ISFORMULA?				
2	5	FALSE				
3	=2+2					
4	hello					
5	=SUM(F2:F6)					
6						

Step 1: In cell B2 enter the formula "**=ISFORMULA(A2)**".

Here is how the formula works:

- Cell A2 is used as the reference argument.

- Excel evaluates the contents of cell A2 to determine whether it contains a formula or not.

- If cell A2 contains a formula, the function will return a value of TRUE.

- If cell A2 does not contain an error, the function will return a value of FALSE.

173

Step 2: Press **Enter**. The result in cell B2 will be FALSE, since cell A2 does not contain a formula.

B2			×	✓	f_x	=ISFORMULA(A2)	

▲	A	B	C	D	E	F
1	Data	ISFORMULA?				
2	5	FALSE				
3	=2+2	TRUE				
4	hello	FALSE				
5	=SUM(F2:F6)	TRUE				
6						

Step 3: Copy the formula down to cell B5. The results in cells B3 and B5 will be TRUE, since cells A3 and A5 contain formulas, while the result in cell B2 and B4 will be FALSE, since these cells do not contain a formula.

To Summarise

The Excel ISFORMULA function is a useful tool for identifying which cells in a range contain formulas. By using this function, you can quickly and easily determine which cells are being calculated based on other cells in your worksheet. This can be particularly helpful when working with large datasets or complex formulas.

ISNUMBER Function

What is it?

The Excel ISNUMBER function is a logical function that checks whether a given value is a numeric value or not. It returns TRUE if the value is a number, and FALSE if it is not.

Syntax

=ISNUMBER(value)

Arguments

- **value** (required): This specifies the value or cell reference that you want to test. It can be any type of value, including a number, text, or logical value.

Example:

Let's say we have a list of values in column A in an Excel worksheet and we want to check which ones are numbers using the ISNUMBER function and display the results in column B.

	A	B	C
1	Data	ISNUMBER?	
2	10		
3	apple		
4	2.5		
5	banana		
6	1000		
7			

Here are the steps to do this:

B2					fx	=ISNUMBER(A2)		

	A	B	C	D	E	F
1	Data	ISNUMBER?				
2	10	TRUE				
3	apple					
4	2.5					
5	banana					
6	1000					
7						

Step 1: In cell B2 enter the formula "**=ISNUMBER(A2)**".

Here is how the formula works:

- Cell A2 is used as the value argument.

- Excel evaluates the contents of cell A2 to determine whether it is a number or not.

- If cell A2 contains a number, the function will return a value of TRUE.

- If cell A2 does not contain a number, the function will return a value of FALSE.

Step 2: Press **Enter**. The result in cell B2 will return a logical value of TRUE, since cell A2 contains a number.

B2					fx	=ISNUMBER(A2)		

	A	B	C	D	E	F
1	Data	ISNUMBER?				
2	10	TRUE				
3	apple	FALSE				
4	2.5	TRUE				
5	banana	FALSE				
6	1000	TRUE				
7						

Step 3: Copy the formula down to cell B6. The results in cells B2, B4 and B6 will be TRUE, since cells A2, A4 and A6 contain a number, while the result in cell B3 and B5 will be FALSE, since these cells contain text.

To Summarise

The ISNUMBER function in Excel is a useful tool for checking if a value is a number or not. By using this function, you can quickly identify which values in a column are numeric and which ones are not. This function can be particularly helpful when working with large data sets, as it can save you time and effort by automating the process of identifying numeric values. Overall, the ISNUMBER function is a simple but powerful feature in Excel that can help you work with data more efficiently and effectively.

ISEVEN Function

What is it?

The Excel ISEVEN function is a built-in function that returns TRUE if the supplied number is even, and FALSE otherwise. It is particularly useful when working with large datasets that require filtering or sorting based on even or odd values.

Syntax

=ISEVEN(number)

Arguments

- **number** (required): The value or cell reference that you want to test if it is even.

Example:

Suppose we have a list of values in column A as shown below:

	A	B	C
1	Data	ISEVEN?	
2	2		
3	7		
4	10		
5	-4		
6	0		
7	5		
8			

We want to check which ones are even numbers using the ISEVEN function and display the results in column B. Here are the steps to do this:

	A	B	C	D	E	F	G
	B2			▼	⋮ ✕ ✓	fx	=ISEVEN(A2)
1	Data	ISEVEN?					
2	2	TRUE					
3	7						
4	10						
5	-4						
6	0						
7	5						
8							

Step 1: In cell B2 enter the formula "=**ISEVEN(A2)**".

Here is how the formula works:

- The number argument is cell A2.

- Excel evaluates the contents of cell A2 to determine whether it is an even number or not.

- If cell A2 is an even number, the function will return a value of TRUE otherwise it will return FALSE.

Step 2: Press **Enter**. The result should be TRUE since 2 is an even number.

	A	B	C	D	E	F	G
	B2			▼	⋮ ✕ ✓	fx	=ISEVEN(A2)
1	Data	ISEVEN?					
2	2	TRUE					
3	7	FALSE					
4	10	TRUE					
5	-4	TRUE					
6	0	TRUE					
7	5	FALSE					
8							

Step 3: Copy the formula down to cell B7. The results in cells B2, B4, B5 and B6 will be TRUE, since cells A2, A4, A5 and A6 contain an even number, while the result in cell B3 and B7 will be FALSE, since cells A3 and A7 contain odd numbers.

Note: The ISEVEN function rounds down any decimal values to the nearest whole number before testing for evenness. Also, if the supplied argument is not a valid number or is a text value, the ISEVEN function returns the #VALUE! error.

To Summarise

The Excel ISEVEN function is a useful tool for determining whether a given number is even or odd. By following the simple steps outlined in this example, you can easily apply the function to your own data and quickly identify which numbers are even and which are odd. This can then be used to filter your dataset.

ISODD Function

What is it?

The Excel ISODD function is a logical function that checks whether a given numeric value is odd or not. It returns TRUE if the number is odd, and FALSE if the number is even.

Syntax

=ISODD(number)

Arguments

- **number** (required): Represents the numeric value that you want to test. It can be a cell reference, a number, or a formula that returns a numeric value.

Example:

Suppose you have a column of numbers in cells A2:A6 and you want to find out which ones are odd and display the results in column B.

	A	B	C
1	Data	ISODD?	
2	2		
3	5		
4	10		
5	13		
6	16		
7			

Here are the steps to do this:

B2   ✕ ✓ *fx* =ISODD(A2)

	A	B	C	D	E	F
1	Data	ISODD?				
2	2	FALSE				
3	5					
4	10					
5	13					
6	16					
7						

Step 1: In cell B2 enter the formula "**=ISODD(A2)**".

Here is how the formula works:

- The number argument is cell A2.

- Excel evaluates the contents of cell A2 to determine whether it is an odd number or not.

- If cell A2 is an odd number, the function will return a value of TRUE otherwise it will return FALSE.

Step 2: Press **Enter**. The result should be FALSE since 2 is an even number.

B2						f_x	=ISODD(A2)	
	A	B	C	D	E	F	G	
1	Data	ISODD?						
2	2	FALSE						
3	5	TRUE						
4	10	FALSE						
5	13	TRUE						
6	16	FALSE						
7								

Step 3: Copy the formula down to cell B6. The results in cells B3, and B5 will be TRUE, since cells A3, and A5 contain an odd number, while the result in cell B2, B4 and B6 will be FALSE, since cells A2, A4, and A6 contain even numbers.

Note: The ISODD function rounds down any decimal values to the nearest whole number before testing for oddness. Also, if the supplied argument is not a valid number or is a text value, the ISODD function returns the #VALUE! error.

To Summarise

This function, like with the ISEVEN function is often used in combination with other functions to perform conditional operations. For example, you can use the ISODD function in an IF statement to check whether a given number is odd or even and then perform an action based on the result.

ISTEXT Function

What is it?

The Excel ISTEXT function is a logical function that returns TRUE if the given value is text, and FALSE if it is not.

Syntax

=ISTEXT(value)

Arguments

- **value** (required): Specifies the value that you want to test. It can be any type of value, such as a number, a date, a logical value, or text. If the value is a text string, the function returns TRUE. If the value is not text, the function returns FALSE.

Example:

Let's say we have a list of values in column A, and we want to check which ones are text and which ones are not and display the results in column B. Here's what our data looks like:

	A	B	C
1	Data	ISTEXT?	
2	Apple		
3	123		
4	Bananas		
5	$4.99		
6	Carrots		
7	10:30		
8	Grapes		
9			

Here is how to do this using the ISTEXT function:

B2				fx	=ISTEXT(A2)		

	A	B	C	D	E	F
1	Data	ISTEXT?				
2	Apple	TRUE				
3	123					
4	Bananas					
5	$4.99					
6	Carrots					
7	10:30					
8	Grapes					
9						

Step 1: In cell B2 enter the formula "**=ISTEXT(A2)**".

Here is how the formula works:

- Cell A2 is used as the value argument.

- Excel evaluates the contents of cell A2 to determine whether it is text or not.

- If cell A2 contains text, the function will return a value of TRUE otherwise it will return FALSE.

Step 2: Press **Enter** to evaluate the formula. The result should be TRUE as this cell contains the text Apple.

B2		▼	⁝	✕	✓	*fx*	=ISTEXT(A2)	
◢	A	B	C	D	E	F		
1	Data	ISTEXT?						
2	Apple	TRUE						
3	123	FALSE						
4	Bananas	TRUE						
5	$4.99	FALSE						
6	Carrots	TRUE						
7	10:30	FALSE						
8	Grapes	TRUE						
9								

Step 3: Copy the formula down to cell B8. As you can see, the ISTEXT function evaluated each value in column A and returned TRUE for the text values, and FALSE for the non-text values.

Note: The ISTEXT function is case-insensitive, which means that it treats uppercase and lowercase letters as the same. For example, =ISTEXT("Hello") and =ISTEXT("hello") both return TRUE. Additionally, if the value argument contains a space character or a formula that returns an empty string (" "), the function returns TRUE.

To Summarise

The Excel ISTEXT function is a simple but powerful tool that can be used to quickly and easily check whether a given value is text or not. This function can be especially useful for data analysis and manipulation, as it allows users to identify and isolate specific types of data in a spreadsheet. By following the step-by-step instructions provided in this example, users can learn how to use the ISTEXT function in Excel and apply it to their own datasets.

ISNONTEXT Function

What is it?

The Excel ISNONTEXT function is a logical function that returns TRUE if the value in a cell is not text, and returns FALSE if the value in a cell is text.

Syntax

=ISNONTEXT(value)

Arguments

- **value** (required): The cell or value that you want to test whether it is non-text. This can be a reference to a cell, a formula, or a value.

Example:

Let's say you have a list of values in cells A2:A6, and you want to check which cells contain non-text values and display the results in column B.

	A	B	C
1	Data	ISNONTEXT?	
2	Apple		
3	25		
4	Pear		
5	45.6		
6	Orange		
7			

Here's how you can use the ISNONTEXT function to do that:

B2   × ✓ *fx*   =ISNONTEXT(A2)

	A	B	C	D	E	F	G
1	Data	ISNONTEXT?					
2	Apple	FALSE					
3	25						
4	Pear						
5	45.6						
6	Orange						
7							

Step 1: In cell B2 enter the formula "**=ISNONTEXT(A2)**".

Here is how the formula works:

- Cell A2 is used as the value argument.

- Excel checks the contents of cell A2 to determine whether it is non-text.

- If cell A2 is non-text, the function will return a value of TRUE otherwise it will return FALSE.

Step 2: Press **Enter** to apply the formula to cell B2. The result will be FALSE, since the value in cell A2 is text.

	A	B	C	D	E	F	G
1	**Data**	**ISNONTEXT?**					
2	Apple	FALSE					
3	25	TRUE					
4	Pear	FALSE					
5	45.6	TRUE					
6	Orange	FALSE					
7							

B2 — fx — =ISNONTEXT(A2)

Step 3: Copy the formula down to cell B6. You will now see that cells B3 and B5 return TRUE, since they contain non-text values (25 and 45.6, respectively), while cells B2, B4, and B6 return FALSE, since they contain text values.

To Summarise

The ISNONTEXT function is a useful Excel function that can be used to identify cells that contain non-text values. By applying the ISNONTEXT function to a range of cells, we can quickly and easily determine which cells contain non-text values and which cells contain text values. This can be helpful in a variety of scenarios, such as when working with data that contains both text and numeric values, or when verifying that data has been entered correctly. The ISNONTEXT function is easy to use and can be a helpful tool for anyone who works with Excel regularly.

CELL Function

What is it?

The Excel CELL function is a built-in function that retrieves information about a cell in a worksheet, such as its formatting, location, and contents.

Syntax

=CELL(info_type, [reference])

Arguments

- **info_type** (required): Specifies the type of information you want to retrieve about the cell. It can be entered as a text string or a reference to a cell that contains the text string. Some examples of info_types are:

    o "address": Returns the cell address in text format, including the sheet name and any dollar signs used to indicate absolute references.

    o "color": Returns a number representing the colour of the cell's interior or font, depending on the optional second argument (see below).

    o "filename": Returns the file name of the workbook containing the cell.

- o "format": Returns the cell's format code.

- o "contents": Returns the contents of the cell.

- o "type": Returns a number representing the data type of the cell (1 for text, 2 for numbers, 4 for logical values, and so on).

- **reference** (optional): Specifies the cell or range of cells you want to retrieve information about. If omitted, Excel uses the cell that contains the formula as the reference. The reference can be entered as a text string or a cell reference.

Example:

Here's an example of how to use the CELL function to retrieve the address of cell.

Step 1: Select a cell to enter the formula to get the cell address. Let's say cell C1.

C1				▼	⋮	✕	✓	*fx*	=CELL("address",A1)
◢	A	B	C	D	E	F	G	H	
1			$A$1						
2									
3									

Step 2: In cell C1, enter the formula "**=CELL("address",A1)**". This formula tells Excel to retrieve the address of cell A1.

Here is how the formula works:

- The CELL function has two arguments: "info_type" and "reference". The "info_type" argument specifies the type of information you want to retrieve about the cell, while the "reference" argument specifies the cell that you want to retrieve the information from.

- In this case, the "info_type" argument is "address", which tells the CELL function to retrieve the address of the cell specified in the "reference" argument.

- The "reference" argument is simply A1, which specifies the cell that we want to retrieve the address of.

Step 3: Press **Enter** to calculate the formula. The value in cell C1 should now be "$A$1", which is the address of cell A1 and the formula returns it as a text string.

Other Examples

You can also use the CELL function to retrieve other types of information about a cell, such as its row number or column letter. Here are a few examples:

- To retrieve the row number of a cell, use the formula: =CELL("row", A1)

- To retrieve the column letter of a cell, use the formula: =CELL("col", A1)

- To retrieve the contents of a cell, use the formula: =CELL("contents", A1)

To Summarise

The Excel CELL function is a useful tool for retrieving information about specific cells in an Excel worksheet. By using the CELL function with different info_type arguments, you can retrieve information such as the address, format, or contents of a cell. In the example provided, we used the CELL function with the "address" argument to retrieve the address of cell A1 demonstrating how this function can be used to retrieve information about a cell's location. With a deeper understanding of how to use the CELL function, you can expand your Excel capabilities and gain more insights from your data.

INFO Function

What is it?

The Excel INFO function is a built-in function that returns information about the current operating environment or current version of Microsoft Excel.

Syntax

=INFO(type_info)

Arguments

- **type_info** (required): Specifies the type of information that you want to retrieve. It can be one of the following values:

  - "directory": Returns the current working directory of the Excel installation.

  - "numfile": Returns the number of worksheets in the active workbook.

  - "origin": Returns the reference style (A1 or R1C1) used in the current Excel installation.

  - "osversion": Returns the version of the operating system running on the computer.

  - "recalc": Returns the calculation mode (automatic, manual, or semi-automatic) used in the current Excel installation.

  - "release": Returns the version number of Excel (for example, "14.0" for Excel 2010).

  - "system": Returns information about the operating system (such as "Windows NT").

Example:

Let's say we want to return the version of the operating system currently running on our computer. Here are the steps to do this:

Step 1: Select a cell to display the version of the operating system. Let's say cell A1.

A1				▾	⋮	✕	✓	*fₓ*	=INFO("OSVERSION")	

◢	A	B	C	D	E	F	G	H
1	Windows (64-bit) NT 10.00							
2								
3								

Step 2: In cell A1, enter the following formula: "**=INFO("OSVERSION")**".

Here is how the formula works:

- The formula works by calling the INFO function, which is a built-in Excel function.

- The function takes one argument, which specifies the type of information to return. In this case, we're passing the argument "OSVERSION", which requests information about the operating system version.

Step 3: Press **Enter** to calculate the formula. The cell will display the version of the operating system.

To Summarise

The INFO function in Excel is a built-in function that allows users to retrieve information about the current operating environment. By passing different arguments to the function, users can retrieve information such as the current operating system version, the current user name, and the version of Excel being used. This function can be useful in various situations, such as when troubleshooting or when working with different versions of Excel or different operating systems.

ERROR.TYPE Function

What is it?

The Excel ERROR.TYPE function is a built-in function that allows you to identify the type of error in a formula. It returns an integer that corresponds to the error type of the cell reference specified.

Syntax

=ERROR.TYPE(error_val)

Arguments

- **error_val** (required): This is the cell reference or formula that you want to evaluate. This argument can be a cell reference or a formula that produces an error. The error can be any one of the following: #N/A, #VALUE!, #REF!, #DIV/0!, #NUM!, #NAME?, or #NULL!

The function returns an integer value that corresponds to the error type of the specified cell reference or formula. The following table lists the error types and their corresponding integer values:

Error Type	Integer Value
#NULL!	1
#DIV/0!	2
#VALUE!	3
#REF!	4
#NAME?	5
#NUM!	6
#N/A	7
#GETTING_DATA	8

Example:

Let's say you have a list of errors in column A and you want to return the type of error in column B as shown below:

◢	A	B	C
1	Data	Error Type	
2	#DIV/0!		
3	#N/A		
4	#VALUE!		
5	#REF!		
6	#NAME?		
7	#NULL!		
8			

Here is an example of how to use the ERROR.TYPE function with step-by-step instructions:

B2   × ✓ *fx*   =ERROR.TYPE(A2)

◢	A	B	C	D	E	F	G
1	Data	Error Type					
2	#DIV/0!	2					
3	#N/A						
4	#VALUE!						
5	#REF!						
6	#NAME?						
7	#NULL!						
8							

Step 1: In cell B2 enter the formula "=**ERROR.TYPE(A2)**".

Here is how the formula works:

- The error_val argument is the reference to the cell or formula that contains the error you want to identify. In this case it is cell A2.

- When you enter the ERROR.TYPE formula into cell B2, Excel returns a number that corresponds to the type of error.

Step 2: Press **Enter**. The result should be 2, which corresponds to the #DIV/0! error.

B2					f_x	=ERROR.TYPE(A2)	
	A	B	C	D	E	F	G
1	Data	Error Type					
2	#DIV/0!	2					
3	#N/A	7					
4	#VALUE!	3					
5	#REF!	4					
6	#NAME?	5					
7	#NULL!	1					
8							

Step 3: Copy the formula in cell B2 all the way through to cell B7. As you can see, the formula returns the integers for all the different error types in column A.

Below are the error types and what they mean:

- 1 - #NULL!: indicates that a formula references a cell range that includes a NULL value (i.e., a blank cell) within its range.

- 2 - #DIV/0!: indicates that a formula attempts to divide a number by zero (0).

- 3 - #VALUE!: indicates that a formula contains an invalid data type, such as trying to perform a calculation on a cell that contains text instead of a number.

- 4 - #REF!: indicates that a formula contains an invalid cell reference, such as a cell that has been deleted or moved.

- 5 - #NAME?: indicates that a formula contains an unrecognised text string or function name.

- 6 - #NUM!: indicates that a formula contains a numeric value that is too large or too small for Excel to handle.

- 7 - #N/A: indicates that a value is not available to a function or formula.

To Summarise

The ERROR.TYPE function in Excel is a useful tool for identifying the type of error in a cell or formula. It returns a number that corresponds to a specific error type, such as #DIV/0!, #N/A, #VALUE!, #REF!, #NAME?, #NUM!, or #NULL!. By using the ERROR.TYPE function, you can easily identify the error in your spreadsheet and take appropriate action to fix it. This can help you to save time and ensure that your data is accurate and reliable.

Excel Formulas and Functions Tips and Tricks

This chapter contains some useful tips and tricks to help you become more efficient and productive in Excel when you are working with Excel formulas and functions.

Using the F9 Key to Evaluate a Formula

When you evaluate a formula, Excel replaces the formula with the result of the calculation. You can evaluate a formula easily using the F9 key. When you use the F9 key, Excel replaces the part of the formula that you selected with the calculated result.

Here are the steps to do this:

Step 1: Click on the cell that contains the formula you want to evaluate.

Step 2: Press the **F2** key to enter edit mode for the cell.

Step 3: Select the part of the formula that you want to evaluate.

Step 4: Press the **F9** key to evaluate the selected part of the formula.

Step 5: To exit edit mode, press the **Esc** key.

Show all Cells That Contains a Formula

Here are the steps to show all cells that contain a formula:

Step 1: Select any cell in the worksheet.

Step 2: Press the **F5** key or alternatively press **Ctrl + G** keys to open the **Go To** dialog box.

Step 3: Click on the **Special** button at the bottom left of the dialog box.

Step 4: In the **Go To Special** dialog box that appears, select **Formulas** and click **OK**.

Excel will select all cells in the range that contain formulas.

How to Convert Formulas to Values

Converting formulas to values is useful for the following reasons:

- **Freeze the results**: When you convert formulas to values, you "freeze" the results of your calculations at that moment. This means that the values won't change if you update or delete the data used in the original calculation, providing you with a stable set of results.

- **Reduce file size**: Excel files with many formulas can be large and take a long time to load or save. By converting formulas to values, you reduce the file size, making it easier to manage and share.

- **Protect formulas**: Converting formulas to values can be useful when you want to protect the formulas from being accidentally changed. This is especially helpful if the spreadsheet will be used by others who may not have the knowledge or experience to understand the formulas.

- **Simplify the view**: Formulas can be complex, and it may be difficult to understand what is happening in the calculation. By converting formulas to values, you simplify the view of the data and make it easier to read and analyse.

Here are the step-by-step instructions to convert formulas to values in Excel:

Step 1: Select the cells containing the formulas you want to convert.

Step 2: Copy the selected cells using the keyboard shortcut **Ctrl + C** or right-click and select **Copy**.

Step 3: Right-click on the cell or range of cells where you want to paste the values.

Step 4: From the right-click menu, select **Paste Special**.

Step 5: In the **Paste Special** dialog box, under **Paste**, select **Values**.

Step 6: Click **OK**.

Hiding Formulas in a Worksheet

There are many reasons you may want to hide a formula in an Excel worksheet. Here are some common reasons:

- **Preventing accidental changes**: When you share an Excel file with others, you may not want them to accidentally change the formulas. Hiding formulas ensures that the formulas cannot be easily edited or deleted.

- **Protecting confidential information**: If your Excel file contains sensitive data, such as financial information or personal data, you may not want others to see the underlying formulas. Hiding the formulas helps to protect this information.

- **Improving readability**: If your Excel sheet contains a lot of formulas, it can be difficult to read and understand. By hiding the formulas, you can make the sheet easier to read and navigate.

- **Avoiding errors**: If you have complex formulas in your Excel sheet, they can be prone to errors. Hiding the formulas can help prevent users from accidentally changing them, which can cause errors in your data.

Here are the step-by-step instructions to hide formulas in Excel:

Step 1: Open the Excel file that contains the formulas you want to hide.

Step 2: Select the cells that contain the formulas you want to hide.

Step 3: Right-click on the selected cells and choose **Format Cells** from the context menu.

Step 4: In the **Format Cells** dialog box, go to the **Protection** tab.

Step 5: Check the box next to **Hidden** and click **OK** to close the dialog box.

Step 6: Now, go to the **Review** tab in the Excel ribbon.

Step 7: Click on the **Protect Sheet** button.

Step 8: In the **Protect Sheet** dialog box, enter a password under **Password to unprotect sheet:**.

Step 9: Click **OK** to close the dialog box.

Step 10: Re-enter the password in the **Confirm Password** dialog box and press **OK**.

Step 11: Save the Excel file.

Now, the formula will be hidden from view.

About the Author

Harjit Suman is an Excel and VBA consultant. He has over 10 years' experience in Excel and VBA and has written a range of books, including Amazon best sellers, to pass on his knowledge of Excel to others. He has also provided Excel and VBA consultancy services to small and medium sized companies. An Analyst in a large global organisation, he enjoys playing lots of sports and in particular tennis and football.

Harjit is also the founder and owner of the Excel Master Consultant website which offers information on everything about Excel. In his website you will find:

- Lots of free Excel tutorials and blogs to expand your Excel knowledge.
- Online Excel and VBA courses you can buy.
- An online shop where you can buy Excel books in paperback, Kindle, and eBook formats.

Please check out his website below:

www.excelmasterconsultant.com

Please take a visit and drop him a message. He would love to hear from you.

Unlock Your Excel Passion with Exclusive Merchandise and eBooks!

Discover a world of exclusive Excel-themed products at my shop! Elevate your style with our chic mugs and trendy t-shirts, all designed for the Excel aficionado in you. Dive into expert insights with our curated eBooks for a power-packed spreadsheet journey.

Explore our Collection!

- 🫖 **Mugs**: Sip your creativity with every brew using our Excel-inspired mugs.
- 👕 **T-Shirts**: Wear your love for Excel proudly with our fashionable and comfortable t-shirts.
- 📚 **eBooks**: Unleash the power of Excel with our expertly curated eBooks. Elevate your skills and efficiency to new heights.

Why Choose Us?

- 😎 **Unique Designs**: Stand out with our one-of-a-kind Excel-themed merchandise.
- 💼 **Functional and Stylish**: Our products seamlessly blend utility with style for the modern Excel enthusiast.
- 📚 **Expert Knowledge**: My eBooks are crafted by myself with over 15 years' experience working with Excel, ensuring valuable insights and practical tips.

Don't Miss Out – Excel Now!

Ready to embrace the Excel lifestyle? Visit my shop and discover a world where every click brings you closer to a better, more stylish Excel experience.

👉 **Shop Now**: www.etsy.com/shop/ExcelstoreByHarjit

🫖 Excel Today, Excel Every Day! 🫖

More Books by Excel Master Consultant

Available to buy on Amazon now!

Excel Bible for Beginners Series

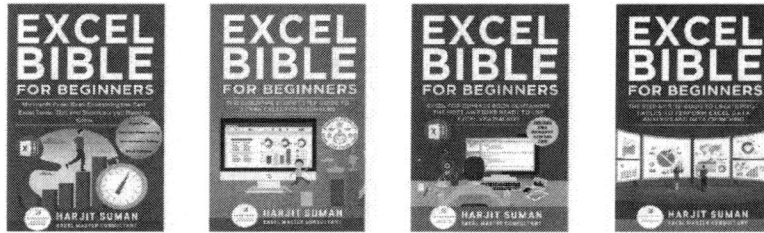

Amazon UK: www.amazon.co.uk/dp/B08C4KVFX3
Amazon US: www.amazon.com/dp/B08C4KVFX3

Excel Formulas and Functions Series

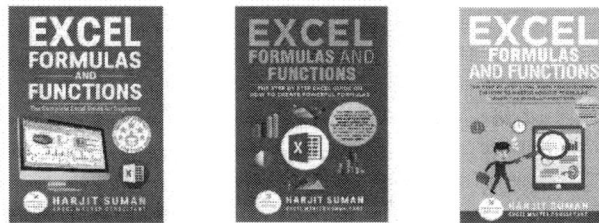

Amazon UK: www.amazon.co.uk/dp/B0868RV3D5
Amazon US: www.amazon.com/dp/B0868RV3D5

Excel 365 Bible Series

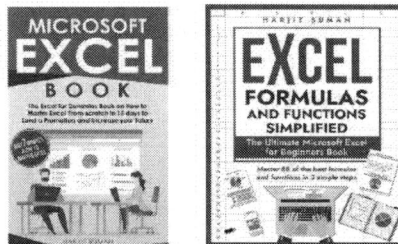

Amazon UK: www.amazon.co.uk/dp/B0B6WQLMF8
Amazon US: www.amazon.com/dp/B0B6WQLMF8

Microsoft Office 365 Book

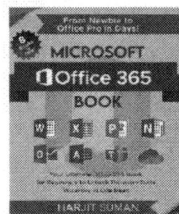

Amazon UK: www.amazon.co.uk/dp/B0CHGBLHYD
Amazon US: www.amazon.com/dp/B0CHGBLHYD

PLEASE LEAVE A REVIEW
What did you think of this book?

First of all, thank you for purchasing this book. I know you could have picked any number of Excel books to read, but you picked this book and for that I am extremely grateful.

I hope that it has improved your Excel skills and you can now confidently use Excel for work and personal use. If so, I would be really grateful if you could share your experience of reading this book with your friends and family by posting to Facebook and Twitter.

If you enjoyed this book, I'd like to hear from you and hope that you could take some time to post a review on Amazon. Your feedback and support will help me to greatly improve my writing craft for future projects and make this book even better.

Your feedback is very important to me and I would be very grateful for your review.

I wish you all the best in your future success and happy Excel learning!

Thank you

Printed in Great Britain
by Amazon